TURNAROUND

Saving a Troubled Business

By: Bob Papes

Cypress Publishing Group, Inc.
11835 Roe # 187
Leawood, KS 66211
www.cypresspublishing.com

Library of Congress Cataloging-in-Publication Data

Papes, Bob
   Turnaround / by Bob Papes

                                      p. cm.
   ISBN: 089447332-8
   1.   Success in business – United States. 2.
      Management – United States. I. Title.

HF5386.A625 2002
658.02′2 — dc20

Printed in the United States of America

10 9 8 7 6 5 4 3 2

In loving memory of John Papes

About the Author

When Bob Papes took on his first business turnaround, there wasn't a manual to help him. He learned like everyone else who has taken on the awesome task of a turnaround — he learned on the job. In his career, Bob has turned around all four businesses that he and his teams have tried to salvage. The turnarounds he and his teams have engineered have been in four different businesses in three different industries.

Bob attended Bellarmine University on an athletic grant-in-aid where he majored in business administration and accounting. While at school, he began to develop his leadership and team skills in student government and on the athletic field. After school, he was recruited into the General Electric Financial Management Training program where he was elected by the 40 trainees of the local training program to be their first president. He spent 19 years with General Electric in various assignments.

With an extensive GE training background, Bob left GE to enter into general management. He has continued to rely on teamwork in the businesses he has run. He has been a general manager for numerous Fortune 500 companies, including ITW, International Paper, James River, American Pad & Paper, and National Service Industries.

His first general manager assignment with a leading paper company was to transform an outdated paper mill, which was producing commodity tissue paper, into a specialty tissue mill. Sales increased by 57% to $23 million and income increased by 73% in one year.

Bob's next turnaround involved a $25 million paper converting plant, which was losing money at the rate of $2 million per year. His team achieved profitability within 12 months. From that assignment, Bob ran an established paper converting business, growing sales by 32% to $29 million in a two-year period, with his team achieving back-to-back record-breaking profits.

Bob then moved on to his third turnaround situation, saving a dying $33 million business, transforming it within one year. In his second full month on the job, his new team achieved current month sales, production, and income records. Income quadrupled in a year.

Most recently, Bob and his new team engineered a fourth turnaround in a completely different industry. The month he arrived, 50% of their sales were transferred to other plants within the company, leaving his new business barely breaking even. Bob and his new team turned a bleak situation into a pre-tax, double digit return on sales (ROS) the following year.

The reason that Bob's teams have been able to consistently turn businesses around is that Bob has focused on his most important resource, people. Through his comprehensive approach of teams, employee involvement, and participative management, Bob's teams have been able to transform multiple businesses, not merely tweak them.

Bob currently serves as the President of the Stretch Sleeve Industry Association. He and his wife, Kay, live in Northeastern Ohio.

Table Of Contents

Section Two
Plugging the Leaks:
Making Operational Changes

Foreword

This book is written for everyone who is faced with one of the most formidable challenges of their career — turning around a business that is failing. Let's be blunt and face the facts: This is one of the most difficult tasks to accomplish. Yes, you can make significant progress. You may stave off the inevitable for a long period, but ultimately the success rate is about 5 to 10%. Before you despair, I want you to know that it can be done. There are certain fundamental things that you can do to significantly increase your odds.

This book is written for those people facing this daunting and complex challenge. It is especially written for:

- Owners who have never run a business for someone else or who have never taken formal leadership training. You see, oftentimes those very traits which got individuals to the point of owning their own businesses, such as great new ideas and creativity, are the very same things which will prevent them from running a business successfully unless they seek help. It seems like a contradiction in terms, but it isn't. Take Steve Jobs at Apple Computer as an example. Starting a business, growing a business, and keeping a business healthy are completely different jobs, requiring different skills.

- New MBAs who have great new skills and learning but who are short on experience. Most of the skills you will need to turn around a business are, for the most part, not taught in graduate schools. Sorry!

- Experienced managers who have been extremely successful at running businesses but never had to salvage a failing one.

- Investment bankers and venture capitalists whose investments are failing and who have to step in and try to do something.

Most of all, this book is written to stop the slide of manufacturing in the United States. While some Fortune 500 companies have the resources to support manufacturing operations in order to make them successful, the truth is that most manufacturing in the U.S. is being done without the kind of talent and leadership that will preserve its future. More and more, occupations have shifted to the service sector, and manufacturing is now comparatively in the minority in the United States. There has to be a reason for this development.

If the U.S. is still the overall technology leader in the world, why is manufacturing dying? Is it because the American worker is lazy and doesn't want to work hard? I say no way! Is it because U.S. companies haven't reinvested the capital necessary to keep our plants competitive? The answer here is dependant upon the industry. You can certainly make that case in the steel industry. To have our manufacturing fade across the board, however, is indicative that something else is wrong, something down to the basic core. W. Edwards Deming, a leader in the Total Quality Management movement to rebuild America's industry after World War II, gave us the ability to compete on quality with the best in the world. Quality in our manufacturing industries has improved immensely during the past ten years. The rebirth of the American automobile industry after the 1970s and early 80s is a case in point. While you can look at a company here and there which has quality problems, the cause of our overall decline in manufacturing is not attributable to quality.

What then can cause such widespread malaise? The answer, in a nutshell, is lack of leadership. While American industry has invested heavily in quality programs such as ISO 2000 and new technology, the truth is that only a few large companies have invested in developing managers and supervisors into leaders. This is why most manufacturing employees hate their jobs and their supervisors.

Most supervisors on manufacturing plant floors have had little or no formal leadership or people skills training. Most manufacturing companies' upper management, plant managers, and supervisors do not have the functioning capability to effectively build and lead teams as well as manage people in a way that will utilize the knowledge and capabilities of their employees.

There are many examples of companies who have transformed themselves into businesses that are people and team oriented. However, for every one business that has heavily invested in the development of their people, there are ten who have not. Most companies will invest in training employees to operate equipment but will not invest heavily in training managers and supervisors to lead and manage their people. They will not invest in the development and training of teams.

This is my hypothesis as to why manufacturing in the United States is declining. It follows that the lack of leadership at the ground level has caused the enormous advantage of our technology to go untapped. Instead, top management has sought a quick fix and opted for the allure of cheap labor overseas. Why aren't the majority of companies developing their people into good leaders? It is because the top managers of most businesses have never had to do it themselves. Most of them got where they are without formal leadership, team building, and people skills training. They ask themselves, if they got where they are without it, why do their people need it, especially when there are appealing offshore alternatives?

After the longest period of prosperity in recent history, manufacturing in America has gone through a recession. The Purchasing Manager's Index, which fell to 41.2 in January 2001, recovered to 55.6 in March 2002. While we are recovering from the recession, our economy cannot continue to prosper if we cannot manufacture the core products needed to fuel growth. The fact that we now have a "service sector" economy is alarming because we have become dependent upon the third world to keep our economy going.

The balance of trade deficits cannot continue indefinitely. We as a country must reverse this devastating trend. How can the owners, CEOs, COOs, general managers, and plant managers running manufacturing businesses save them and their employees' jobs? Loans, tariffs, and surcharges are all "band-aids," not permanent fixes. It is going to take experienced leadership as well as an integrated process of "operational fixes" to achieve this turnaround. Are there specific leadership characteristics and practices and a defined process of "operational fixes" which successfully turn businesses around? Yes!

In each of the four businesses that I have been fortunate to be able to turn around, the cause was the same — leadership at the local business unit level. This is too much of a coincidence. This book is based on my real-life experiences. It is based upon the things that I have done that have repeatedly worked in each of the four turnaround challenges.

In *Turnaround*, I share my real-life turnaround experiences and learning. Some managers are fortunate to be able to engineer one dramatic business turnaround in their careers. By utilizing teamwork as a foundation, my teams and I have engineered four consecutive turnarounds. The real difference with this book is that instead of just telling what to do, I explain *how* to do it. *Turnaround* gives real examples and explanations of how to go about turning a business around as well as the reasons for doing it.

If you are looking for a fail-safe formula for turning a business around, forget it. There is no such thing because the circumstances are different in every situation. Different circumstances require different actions and fixes. The good news, however, is that there is a systematic approach you can take to assess what needs to be done as well as ways of managing that will greatly enhance your chances of success. With a historical success rate of somewhere from 5 to 10%, you are going to need all the help you can get.

It is appalling what many Fortune 500 companies consider "strategies to fix businesses." These strategies, without fail, can be reduced to two plans: cut heads and count paper clips. Naturally, you must cut costs to stop the bleeding, but cutting costs, and only cutting costs, does not cure the cancer that has invaded the patient and threatened its existence. Yet, time after time I've seen this as *the* action plan in America's leading companies. So here is my first rule: **You cannot "cost reduce" enough in order to save the business. If that is all you do, you will fail.**

A story will illustrate this point well. Early in my career, I worked for a Fortune 500 consumer electronic business. The television business was losing millions. They tried the cost reduction routine, moving a lot of their operations to Singapore and closing a plant manufacturing their cabinets for console televisions. While these actions helped, it didn't make the company profitable. Then one day, another mid-level sales manager and I started talking.

This manager was responsible for the private label business within the company. Our general manager was not inclined to go after this market because of its low profit margins. As the manager of Marketing Operations Analysis, he asked for my help. I figured we had nothing to lose, so I looked into it. What I discovered was that we were comparing private label margins to retail margins, or as they say, comparing apples to oranges.

The really big difference was that private label sales didn't incur a lot of the costs that the retail sales channel did, such as labor warranty, outbound transportation, volume rebates, inventory financing charges, advertising costs, and the cost of our share of a national sales force. When I did an estimated income statement before income taxes, I saw that the private label business was profitable and the retail segment was in the red. We brought this analysis to our finance manager and our general manager and convinced them that we could grow the private label segment without adding many of the costs associated with the retail segment. They bought into the concept. We began growing the private label segment by leaps and bounds. They eventually grew the private label sales to more than $100,000,000 a year, and the total business began to make money.

I will never forget shaking my head at the number of salaried people in that business, making a good wage, who had a severe case of the 9-to-5 syndrome. While I'm not suggesting that everyone should have put in the hours I did, I learned a lot about turning around a business at an early age. When you are fighting to save a business, there is no place for the luxury of "normal hours." There is not a lot of time or money that can be wasted, and if you make the wrong decision, the company may die an early death. Saving a company is not a job for the faint of heart or indecisive people. It is a job with enormous responsibility that requires the right decisions to be made.

When you go to a seminar or read a management book, you get a bunch of "what to do's." Rarely do you get the "how to do" of what must be done. This book is the rare exception. It will, I hope, give you both. It delivers on this promise because it is written from the best perspective of all—actual experience.

I was blessed to have worked with some wonderful people in my career. My role was to energize them, give them direction, and support and get them going. You have to have good people to save a dying business. These people are very special to me, and I think of them often. They are too numerous to try and name in this book. I am eternally grateful for their help and support.

To all those people who have helped me in my career, I say thank you. I want to give a special thanks to:

- Don Perry
- Dexter Hagy
- Frank Ritgert
- Jack Campbell

I want to give a special acknowledgement to the following people who helped me with this work. Their contributions were enormous.

- Dr. Kathleen Razzi
- Rich Papes
- George Valaika
- Peter Tourtellot

To those individuals taking on a turnaround for the first time, I hope these tidbits of knowledge will help you be successful. I wish you the best. For those of you in the manufacturing field, the future of manufacturing as well as the future of our country is riding on how well you do.

So, come with me on a journey, one that will enlighten, shock, frighten, and amuse you. One thing I can promise you—after reading this book, you will be better prepared than I was when I tackled my first turnaround situation and my job and the future of my business were on the line. You will also learn what to ask and what to evaluate before you take on this formidable challenge.

Section One

Laying the Foundation:

Instituting New Leadership

CHAPTER ONE

YOU GET "THE CALL"

You can get "the call" to step into a turnaround situation in many ways. Sometimes, the turnaround is a job you didn't ask for or expect. Your boss, for example, gives you a promotion, and you haven't the slightest idea what you're getting into. You change jobs and take the position without being told the truth, the whole truth and nothing but the truth. You can also willingly take it on as a crusader, a knight in shining armor.

The truth is that only one of the four companies that hired me to turn their business around painted an accurate picture of how bad a condition they were in at the time. This is a result of several factors. One is that while they know the financials, they don't really know what is causing the problem and don't know how to fix it. If they did know, they probably wouldn't need you. They may know, for example, that more sales are needed. However, they probably don't know why these additional sales aren't being generated. Since they don't know, they can only give you their perceptions of what is wrong. They may know that they are in trouble but not understand the full scope of the problem. Very often, they are oblivious to the true nature of the problem until it is overwhelming and the boat is sinking.

It may be that they don't want to tell you how bad the situation really is. They fear that if a candidate really knew the extent of the problem, the chances of retaining a highly skilled, qualified person would diminish. Why would a great candidate jeopardize his or her career or willingly take on such a task? Still another reason is that hiring managers do not want their bosses to know how bad it is, which would thereby draw blame to themselves. They want to downplay the disaster and simply hope that you can make it go away quickly, as though they never let things get out of control.

Before you can do anything, you must get a handle on the financials and what the budget is for this or the next year and then assume that the ship is going down a lot faster than what you are hearing. Typically, you are only shown the tip of the iceberg.

There are some things you should try and assess as best you can during the interview. Probe your potential new bosses as to what their expectations are to fix the business. Try to pin them down to a specific time frame and what a successful turnaround would look like to them. Also, spend time probing your new bosses' philosophy about key approaches to fix businesses, such as teams, Total Quality Management, employee involvement, empowerment, or their perceptions of the capabilities of the management and supervision.

You must realize that businesses that are failing need to be totally transformed, not merely changed. This means that you have to grab and shake the business down to its very core. When you do this, you are going to step on toes and anger a lot of people. You are going to run into resistance. People will actively backstab you, speaking ill of you to your boss. You must have the support of your boss to do what you have to do, even though going in he or she probably doesn't accurately understand what really needs to be done. I wouldn't have been able to accomplish any turnaround without the help and support of top management. Before you accept a job to turn around a business, you need to know that you will be completely supported at the very top. Assessing that is probably the single most important decision you have to make.

In a previous assignment, I had a long discussion about teams and employee involvement with a president of a company during my final interview. I left the interview feeling that he was a very progressive leader and that he would support my efforts to transform the company. I was offered the job and accepted the position.

When I formed teams, started training them, and began having team meetings, the president, the division HR manager, and the division controller all came down to have a talk with me. The president indicated to me that we couldn't afford to hold team meetings. I explained to him that one of the critical characteristics of a team was active communication, planning, and problem solving. His response was that we couldn't afford that.

To my shock and dismay, his concept of a team was merely to buy employees t-shirts and tell them that they were a team. While he had read of teams, he had never run a plant with teams and didn't have any idea what was involved. I told him that we would end up with work groups and not teams. He said, "That is what I want."

Despite having discussed my philosophy in detail during the interview, I did not really find out his true beliefs until after I accepted the job. The best way to find out whether your potential new boss "walks the walk" is to talk to general managers, presidents, and COOs of other businesses under him or her. Remember, an ounce of prevention is worth a pound of cure. Do your homework, and don't get yourself into a situation like Joan of Arc found herself in; her boss was afraid of her growing influence, her philosophy was foreign to him, and he sent her into battle without the promised support. The rest is history.

If you want to be able to "right the ship," upper management must give you the support to do what has to be done. This will make a difference, not only in being successful but also in how happy you will be doing the job.

About the best you can realistically hope for is to right the ship in one year. Righting the ship means getting it out from under water. It does not mean that it will be operating at full steam and highly competitive. Why use a timeline of one year? We will discuss the reasons later on in this book. You have to realize that a failing business has many fundamental problems that must be corrected. There are no lasting quick fixes. On the other hand, business turnarounds cannot be accomplished through gradual, incremental change. Change has to be fundamental, and it has to be swift. A balance is needed. You must plow the field, plant good seed, and fertilize and nurture your crop before there can be any harvest.

If you cannot get that kind of commitment out of your potential new boss, run from the job. Don't walk, don't dawdle — otherwise you might get sucked in. Your chances for success are very slim, even if you do everything right. You have no chance unless your boss has a realistic expectation of what resources are needed and how long it will take.

The biggest hurdle in turning a business around is usually the management for whom you will be working. They don't teach you that in business school. First of all, if the business is in trouble, who got it there? If they were doing their jobs well, why don't they have a qualified internal candidate to fill the position? The biggest issue, however, is that in most companies upper management cannot correctly assess the effectiveness of the new manager that they have hired without resorting to inappropriate techniques. Most bosses go and talk to your people behind your back. The more desperate and paranoid they get, the more likely they are to place "spies" in your organization. They will institute an informal reporting system in which they will get information from your people, often before you do. In this environment, your authority is compromised before you begin. None of the bosses I have had utilize 360-degree reviews.

Instead, they will usually go behind you directly or indirectly. The indirect path is usually from one of your people to a division or group staff member who is part of the old culture. The division or group managers often work hard at developing moles in your organization. The most likely mole will be the controller.

If you have people who have not been doing a good job and you are holding them accountable for their performance, do you think you are going to be very popular? Yet, that is exactly what most upper-level managers look for, except they call it "fitting in." If you are well liked, you "fit in." Most upper-level managers, unfortunately, may not have an effective way to correctly assess the leadership of people who run their businesses. Most of them also do not know how to turn a business around, and most have never had to do it themselves.

Do not make the mistake that they will give you an objective, unbiased assessment. They will not intentionally be unfair. They simply do not know how to do it and tend to utilize feedback from people with whom they are "comfortable." These same people are usually part of the establishment. In this way, feedback tends to come from the people in your organization who are resisting the changes that you are trying to make and who therefore have negatively biased opinions!

If everyone likes you, you are not effecting the transformation of the business that is required of you. If you are successfully transforming the business, not everyone will like you. This will hurt you with some bosses. An important question to ask the company that is hiring you is how they will assess the job that you are doing and how well your leadership is working.

Pin them down as to what they will look for in your leadership and how they will assess it. Specifically ask them if they will question your people about you or not. You must get an agreement on how they will assess your leadership. If you cannot get a specific commitment from your potential new bosses, walk away. The backstabbing will kill you, and you will never know what is happening.

Summary

There is no question that it is essential to have a supportive boss who believes in what you are doing and, more importantly, the way you are doing it. If you are to be successful, you must be working for someone who will support the tough decisions that you must make.

Remember that the key reason most failing businesses are failing is because either the upper management isn't willing to do the really tough things that need to be done or because they cannot accurately assess what needs to be done. In either case, turning it around will require their support. The key is to ask enough tough questions in your interviews to assess which is really the case and how committed they really are to improving the business.

Now that you have been coached on what to sort out with the hiring managers, the next step you must take before accepting the position is to complete an extensive self-assessment. We will discuss this in the next chapter.

Chapter One
Workbook

- Have you and your new/potential boss identified the key issues which *he or she* feels need to be addressed? If so, what are they?

_____

_____

_____

_____

- Have you and your new/potential boss identified the time it is expected to take to turn the business around? What is it?

_____

_____

_____

_____

- Did you and your new/potential boss agree to specifics in terms of what success will look like? Did the two of you agree to quantitative goals? If so, what are they?

_____

_____

_____

_____

CHAPTER TWO

LEADERSHIP

Unquestionably the most important skill one must possess to successfully transform a business is leadership. Leadership is a very ambiguous word. It means different things to different people. This is probably why it is rarely ever assessed as part of the interviewing process. Yet without good leadership skills, revitalizing a failing business is impossible.

The truth is that the type of leadership needed really depends upon the development level of the organization. It is critical to make an assessment of the level of the organization first to decide which leadership style will be most effective. For example, if you have a bunch of young, ambitious workers with little experience, you must give them direction and monitor their progress. They will probably be long on enthusiasm and short on good judgment. If you have an organization full of people who have never been empowered, empowering them and expecting immediate results without developing them will be both frustrating and potentially devastating to your career.

Some of the key elements you need to assess in your organization's workforce are:

- **Competence**

  How much specific job knowledge or know-how do they have? How much experience do they have?

- **Commitment**

  What is their amount of motivation? What is their amount of effort and personal sacrifice?

- **Character**

The answers to these questions will guide you to the type of leadership style you need to employ in order to affect change. Utilizing a style that will not be effective with the development level of your troops will only frustrate them and you. Before you wade into the swamp, step back and assess the landscape. What do you see in terms of the three key elements above?

One of my manufacturing managers leading a team with low commitment and variable competence let his team meet by themselves and work on a predetermined issue. After six months, they had gotten nowhere, and he was frustrated. Had he understood ahead of time that they wouldn't be able to effectively move forward without his involvement and coaching, they would have made good progress, felt good about themselves, and made a significant contribution to the organization.

I once had a sales manager who tried managing his sales representatives in an autocratic manner. His representatives had high commitment but low competence. This scenario would indicate that he should manage them in a directive style (i.e., by telling them exactly what they needed to do and how to do it). He couldn't, however, differentiate the need for a directive management style versus an autocratic one (where he issued demands but didn't specify how they were to be accomplished). As a result, he demoralized his sales force. Matching your leadership style to the develop-ment level of your people is critical in order to maximize your effectiveness and the effectiveness of the organization.

One of the most difficult things to learn is that while you must treat people the same, you cannot deal with them in the same way! It is imperative that you treat all people fairly and with dignity and respect. You cannot, however, lead and manage them all in the same way using the same techniques. Some need to be given direction; some need to be given coaching; some need to be given support; while with others, you need to simply give them the task and get out of their way. The real trick is to know which employees require which type of leadership.

Is there a foolproof test that you can give so that you can make that determination? Probably not—the best way I know of is to spend time with them, both one on one as well as in meetings. You are never going to be sure, but you must at least make a decision. The other way is to test them by giving small, limited assignments and judging the results. Sometimes a small task will yield big payoffs in insight into your staff members.

It is important that you reassess your style on a periodic basis. People react to different situations in different ways, and thus it is essential that you gauge the style that it necessary and appropriate. Using a leadership style that takes into account the situation and people involved will help improve productivity and efficiency.

Choosing the right leadership style is crucial to saving the business. You will have to choose one style for your leadership team, but you will have to utilize multiple styles when dealing with each teammate individually. They will be at varying levels of development, so you must vary your style with each member.

No matter what kind of leadership style is needed, it must come from someone whom the people will follow. The best definition of leadership I have learned comes from the Georgia-Pacific Corporation:

> **Leadership is the capacity to engage with others, drawing upon one's own motives, values, and beliefs while tapping the motives, values and beliefs of others so as to develop a shared vision of the future which mobilizes human resources and elevates expectations channeled toward a common purpose.**

A key to being successful is to know the difference between leading and managing. Don't feel bad if you don't know the difference at the present time, most experienced managers don't. At times there is a fine line between the two. There can be huge differences or minor ones.

The best way I know of to think of leadership versus managing is to put these dynamics in a model. The P.D.R.C. Model is as good an explanation of the differences between managing and leading as I have come across. When I worked for James River Paper Company, now a part of Georgia-Pacific Corporation, they employed the P.D.R.C. model. The "P" stands for **Purpose,** the "D" stands for **Direction,** the "R" stands for **Regulation,** and the "C" stands for **Capability.**

P.D.R.C. MODEL

Purpose	**D**irection	**R**egulation	**C**apability
Vision	Strategy	Commitment	Grow
LEADERSHIP is above the line			
Mission	Plans	Conformance	Sustain
	MANAGEMENT is below the line		
Goals	Methods	Control	Operate

Reprinted with permission from Georgia-Pacific Corporation.

Each category is divided into three key segments. When you are functioning above the diagonal line in the model, you are leading. When you are functioning below the diagonal line, you are managing.

Now that you have a basic understanding of the difference, you ask, "Which should I be doing?" The answer is *both!* You cannot just do one or the other and be successful. You must spend time on both styles. The simple truth is that most managers spend 95% of their time trying to manage. This is why so many businesses are unsuccessful. You must balance leadership and management.

Circumstances may dictate that you spend more time operating above or below the line at any one point in time. The important thing is that you know where you are operating and why and that you control how long you spend in that mode. The capacity to lead an organization requires that you develop the skills and traits that characterize the categories above the line. If you do not, you are just fighting fires as they crop up. While some emergency management is definitely necessary, if that is all you do, you will become exhausted and the business will burn to the ground.

Character

So what then are the key personal characteristics necessary to lead well and to gain people's commitment? (Notice I said commitment and not capitulation.) As usual, there is not just one but several factors.

It takes an extraordinary amount of character to turn a business around. The key leadership character trait is trustworthiness. Trust is the cornerstone of the foundation you must build in order to save the business. Trust must be earned; it cannot be demanded. In order to earn people's trust, you must have the right leadership characteristics that allow workers to trust in you and follow you willingly. Just what are the characteristics of trust?

Do what you say you will do. Do you tell people what they want to hear or do you level with them and follow through on what you said you would do? Consistency between your actions and words lets people know what is expected of them and what the consequences are for failing to meet expectations. You will also be setting an example of honesty, accountability, and dependability that will encourage employees to act in the same manner. For example, if you indicate that people using drugs will be terminated, don't start making exceptions or you will lose your credibility.

Treat people with dignity and respect. You cannot treat people with respect if you are yelling at them or, worse yet, swearing and cussing at them. Do not behave or speak condescendingly. Get to know all your workers by name, everyone from the very top of the organization to the very bottom. Acknowledge them. Show an interest in them. Do not shoot the messenger and blame the one who brings you news that you don't want to hear. Be approachable and listen to people and their ideas, even when they differ from your own. You must be sincerely interested in what they have to say. More importantly, you must be willing to try to utilize their suggestions. By reaffirming people's ideas, you are reaffirming them. This says that you believe in them, value them, and have confidence in their ability.

You must be consistent and fair. This is really hard to do at times, but that is why being a good leader is tough. Not many people want to be held to such high standards. Yet it is critically important. You cannot treat people differently. If people perceive that you have favorites, your creditability and trustworthiness will go down quicker than a bungee jumper without a cord.

You must be open and honest. If people perceive that you are intentionally misleading them, their trust will evaporate overnight. Remember what happened to President Clinton when the public learned he "misled" them? Being honest means more than just telling the truth. It means not leaving out key elements of the story. It means being willing to discuss "uncomfortable" things and being approachable. It means that just because you're the boss, you will not be held to different rules or expectations than other employees. What's more, you are held to higher standards because you are the ultimate example for the entire organization.

If you can consistently operate under these trust-building traits, 99% of the time you will be able to earn people's trust. The first and foremost challenge is recognizing that as the leader of the business, you must work to earn people's trust. The second challenge is to make the sacrifices and put forth the effort to accomplish this essential step.

Before you embark on any turnaround, you must first assess whether or not you possess these characteristics. If you are young and do not have the experience of having been put through the test on the job, the best way to find out is to go to a respected psychological testing firm that specializes in employment evaluation or career profiling. If you're serious about taking on a turnaround, it is worth the investment of time and money to find out what your strengths are and where you need to improve.

There are many different kinds of profiles. They measure different attributes, such as dominance, influence, steadiness, patience, problem solving, etc. Tests such as the Myers-Briggs personality test may not be as useful as other types of tests because it is more focused on how you interact than your particular personality strengths. If you are to be an effective turnaround artist you need to have a high level of personal drive and a strong desire to influence or shape your environment. The most successful people also have a good ability to influence others.

Even if you are an experienced manager, get honest feedback from your confidants. Don't just ask them if you are a good leader! Have your HR manager survey people who work directly under you about your character. Collaborate with your HR manager in designing the survey and then have your direct reports turn the survey into the HR manager so that he or she can compile it anonymously. Investigate whether or not they see you as open and honest. Ask open-ended questions, not ones that can be answered yes or no and which provide little usable information.

Summary

If your self-assessment comes up short, don't despair. These skills can be learned but not in a turnaround situation. If you don't have them, run! Do not be tempted to take it on no matter how tempting the pay. The odds of failure are overwhelming. While paying for a good evaluation of your character is expensive, failing at running a turnaround can be devastating to your career. Don't put yourself in that position.

So if you have these character traits and the right attitude, you are ready to take on the turnaround job, right? Well, maybe and maybe not. What other traits will you need in order to be successful? That is the focus of our next chapter.

Chapter Two
Workbook

- How would you describe your leadership style?

_____

_____

_____

_____

_____

- Where do you spend most of your time in the four vertical categories of the P.D.R.C. model? Place a check in the appropriate category. What does this say about your leadership/management style?

Purpose	Direction	Regulation	Capability
__Vision	__Strategy	__Commitment	__Grow
__Mission	__Plans	__Conformance	__Sustain
__Goals	__Methods	__Control	__Operate

_____

_____

_____

_____

_____

- Ask three of your peers/direct reports to fill out how they see your profile on the P.D.R.C. model. Have them send this profile to HR and have HR prepare a composite rating for you. How closely does their profile match your own perceptions? If they see you differently from how you see yourself, what changes in your style do you intend to make?

_____

_____

_____

_____

- Do you feel you need to change your style in order to effectively engineer a turnaround? If so, what changes do you intend to make? How do you intend to do it?

_____

_____

_____

_____

- Have you taken a personality/behavioral profile? If so, what did it tell you?

_____

_____

_____

- Do you feel your profile will enable you to successfully engineer a turnaround? If not, do you feel you can effectively change your profile? If not, should you take on this assignment?

_____

_____

_____

_____

CHAPTER THREE
OTHER KEY CHARACTERISTICS

After reading the last chapter, you may be saying, "You mean I need more than good leadership to do the job? What else do I need?" The answer, unfortunately, is plenty. While there isn't any magic formula, here are key characteristics at the top of my list for a successful turnaround:

- **Leadership**
- **Courage**
- **High energy and motivation**
- **Competence and technical expertise**
- **Heart**

We have already discussed leadership. Now, I will share my insights on the other key characteristics.

Courage

Sounds like something out of a novel, right? It isn't. I am not going to try and define it for you. Rather, I am going to give you examples of what kind of courage you will need; you can decide for yourself whether or not you can deal with it. Keep in mind that these things happened in turnaround situations where the business was already fighting for survival. The good news is that we managed to overcome these setbacks. However, I did not know at the time that we would be able to overcome them. This is where you must have the toughness of character to overcome the sick feeling in the pit of your stomach.

Everyone deals with these overwhelming obstacles differently from an emotional standpoint. Don't ever underestimate how powerfully they will affect your emotional well-being. As for me, when these seemingly insurmountable obstacles rose unexpectedly out of the swamp, I lost many a night's sleep tossing and turning. I had a sick feeling in the pit of my stomach to the point that it actually ached. I often felt physically ill. This is a huge price to pay for having to deal with "stuff" that you are inheriting and didn't cause to happen. Don't ever under-estimate the toll a turnaround can have on you mentally, emotionally, and physically.

While you are going to have problems regardless of what business you are running, a problem in a turnaround situation can cause the ship to sink. It can cause you to fail because there is no buffer of profit to absorb it. Every problem can sink you further into the swamp.

Examples of Courage

 I was on the job less than two weeks when one of my sales reps came and told me that we had just lost our biggest customer. I hadn't even unpacked all my boxes yet, and at that point, I wanted to pack them up and go home. Try as we might, we could not get them to change their minds. The business was already losing money—this was a deathblow. I had to either fight or flee, and I decided to stay. The twelfth month I was there we started making money. Not a whole lot mind you, but we righted the ship.

The lesson here is: Be prepared for serious setbacks. Not everything will go right, especially from the start. Do not despair no matter how bad the situation looks.

 I found out that a new customer in Mexico wasn't paying their bills and owed us $250,000. After 30 days of constant phone calls that were not returned, we found out that they had sold the business. Pass the Rolaids please!

The lesson here is: Failing businesses tend to take too many high risks. Establish review and approval procedures quickly. You can't reverse the bad decisions that were already made, but you can keep from crawling further out on the limb.

 I found out that my sales manager didn't have a clue about how much business we could get from his customers. After doing an in-depth assessment, we concluded that he would miss his sales budget by $1 million or 25% of his budget and 10% of my total sales budget.

The lesson here is: Desperate businesses tend to grasp at straws and take the positive spin on news. Review the important sources of your revenue forecasts and scrutinize them in depth. You will be surprised at what you find.

 I was on the job for about four months when I looked out my window and saw surveyors measuring the parking lot. Since I realized that I hadn't authorized it, I decided to investigate. I discovered that the corporate office had asked my organization for a plethora of data. My heart sank. Two months later they sold the whole company consisting of four plants, including mine.

The lesson here is: The owner wasn't committed to the business and merely used me and my team to enhance the selling price of his business. I don't know what to tell you to look for, except beware of this possibility with companies that are in trouble.

 I worked for an envelope plant that was owned by a major paper company. Not only was I buying paper at the same prices as everyone else, but also the paper sales management was lobbying my upper management to divest our division because we competed with some of their customers. They closed the business less than one year after we had turned it around.

The lesson here is: Know when you don't have the support of management. Without it, you ride a sinking ship down. This won't help anyone, including your career.

 In one turnaround, 50% of our sales evaporated the month I walked in the door. We were making product to support two sister plants offshore. While I knew this was a distinct possibility when I walked in the door, what I didn't know was that there weren't any sales prospects in the pipeline. We had to bring in new business quickly without any starting point.

We managed to bring in more than $3 million in new business that year, which should have put our plant in a tremendous position. Unfortunately, we also lost more than $2 million in existing business, which we did not cause. It was a result of previous poor management and inattention. Instead of having "slain the dragon" with this new business, we had to go back out once again and duplicate securing more new business even though we didn't cause the problem. Doing this under the gun, where the future of the business is in jeopardy, is highly stressful.

The lesson here: When a ship goes down, what you see in front of you is usually the tip of the iceberg. Be sure to look under the surface or you are in for some surprises.

 I managed a plant where a female supervisor was threatened by one of our male employees. She was married with kids and was simply friends with this employee. They would occasionally go to lunch together or have a drink after work. I don't believe it was ever anything more than that.

One day, this employee cursed and swore at our plant manager. The female supervisor observed this behavior and later verified the truth of its occurrence. This resulted in the employee being put on suspension for several days without pay. When he came back to work, he followed her out to the parking lot after work one day. He jumped in the front seat of her car and threatened her. He told her he would "get" her if she kept saying those "bad things" about him. She was shaken by the encounter.

While we dismissed the employee for this behavior, we felt very uneasy for the supervisor's safety, especially as she worked the second shift when management was not around. We decided that her safety was of the utmost importance. She did not want to change shifts for a temporary period of time because of her kids' schedule.

We ended up hiring off-duty policemen, who carried guns, to be in the plant with her during her shift, to meet her in the parking lot, and to walk her to her car after her shift. We did this for about three weeks. Obviously, our workers were very nervous, as was I. It was a high-stress situation but protecting her and dismissing him was the absolute right thing to do.

The lesson here is: A lot of businesses fail because their management won't do the really difficult and uncomfortable things. If having to deal with this type of situation, while clearly unpleasant, is something you would prefer to avoid, stay home. Don't try to take on a turnaround because you will have to deal with many "uncomfortable" issues.

When you are working to successfully resuscitate a business, don't expect to be popular. You must realize going in that the team that got the business into the desperate situation it is in cannot get it out of trouble. You will most likely have to fire some managers and supervisors. In the first year of my last turnaround, I had to replace three of six key managers and all three supervisors.

I could go on with stories on the difficulties of these situations. You get the idea. Leading a turnaround is not for the faint of heart. It requires courage and a level head.

High Energy and Motivation

The third thing you will need for this job is high energy and motivation. Let me say up front that nobody can turn a business around alone. You are going to need the help of the entire team, which will be discussed in a later chapter. Even at that, turning a business around takes enormous dedication. Putting in 60-hour weeks is the norm. If you do not have the health and physical or mental strength to do this for a solid year, don't even bother to take the job.

Even if you are up for it, will your team be? The trick is to energize your team to put forth the same kind of effort. I have been most effective energizing my teams by:

- Conducting leadership meetings in a way that allowed the team to participate in key decisions and make the decisions utilizing true consensus.
- Keeping my leadership team well informed and sharing the financials with them as well as the entire workforce, right down to the plant floor.
- Giving positive reinforcement whenever I could.
- Tying their salary increases directly to performance.
- Mutually establishing fair, objective, and measurable goals that were tied to the turnaround of the business and paying their bonuses on their individual and team results.
- Supporting them in their struggles, removing barriers and obstacles for them, encouraging them, and picking them up, dusting them off, and sending them back into battle.

Competence

You will not get anywhere if you do not have competence. Not only must you possess it, your key managers and supervisors must possess it as well. This includes the technical expertise necessary to do the job well. In a turnaround, you must right the ship quickly. You do not have the luxury of time to develop people or to improve their skills. You must have experienced people you can go to under any circumstances. If you have to do it for them or hold their hand, they will bog you down and you will run out of time and fail. You have got to have good people to save a business. If you are not willing to change out players to get the best employees, stay home. The truth is that the team who led the business into the pit cannot get the business out of it. You will also need the ability to bring a competent leadership team together, to work together effectively, and to trust each other. You must also be able to energize your team. This is no easy task.

Heart

Another key ingredient is heart. My definition of heart is "loving the troops." This means really caring about your workers and being there for them. You must support them when they do a good job and support them even when they make mistakes. It means opening your home to them at Christmas; it means listening to their personal problems; it means attending funeral services of the family of your managers and supervisors; it means knowing all your people on a first-name basis; it means talking to your people on the plant floor and asking them about their sick father, mother or spouse and so on.

People need to know that you care about them on a personal level and view them as more than a disposable cog in a machine. That is not to say that you must be emotionally attached to everyone, which would cloud your objective decision making. However, if you do not care for your employees and demonstrate this concern to them, you will not gain their trust and loyalty. They will probably be less motivated and less productive because they do not view their company or their boss—you being their most visible representative of the company—as being concerned for the well-being of its employees.

If you deal with employees as depersonalized "units," then you run a high probability of dehumanizing your approach. A turnaround cannot work unless you have the support of the staff; you have to earn their respect. It starts by having respect for them as people, not just as "factors of production."

Summary

While the list of key characteristics can be a list as long as your arm, the ones mentioned above are the essential ones. You must have good leadership, exceptional courage, high energy and dedication, have a lot of heart, and be able to build a competent team. You must be able to inspire them and get them to work together effectively, which is no easy task. You will need to make multiple operational changes as well. There is no way to know what these changes will be until you go in and make your assessment. You can, however, assess your own character to see if you have what it takes to be successful. If you possess these characteristics, you will significantly influence the odds for success. Deciding ahead of time whether you have the right characteristics is a critical evaluation you must make. You alone know if you are right for the job. Unfortunately, most managers and the hiring bosses who take on turn-arounds don't even have a clue what to look for in candidates. Now you do! Don't fail to use it.

Chapter Three
Workbook

- What difficult business situations have you had to personally address that tested your character? What were the positive ways in which you approached these situations? What things do you feel you should have done differently?

_____

_____

_____

_____

_____

_____

- Assess the above answer to determine whether or not you have had to face enough adversity to adequately test your character? If so, why? What experience have you gained?

_____

_____

_____

_____

_____

- How well do you feel your character matches up with the key characteristics needed to pull off a turnaround? If they do not match up well, why do you still want to attempt this challenge?

_____

_____

_____

_____

_____

CHAPTER FOUR

WHERE DO I START?

As I said earlier, most companies cut heads and count paper clips. While cost reduction will help your bottom line, it cannot fix it by itself. Cost cutting can prevent you from losing money, but it cannot move you from terminally ill to successful.

Your management will probably expect you to reduce operational expenses and to layoff employees. One school of thought says, "Don't fight them." On the other hand, nothing hurts morale more than indiscriminant layoffs, so use discretion and do not rush into anything. You might end up firing the very people who could help you save the company. So what do you do first, you ask? The answer has two parts.

You must assess the development level of your organization from the top down, doing an "internal evaluation." The problem is that any "inside evaluation" will not tell you the whole picture. The only way you will know what to do is to reach outside the organization. You must talk to customers to find out what you have to do to fix the business. While you will get a lot of opinions from people in your organization as to how to fix the business, the truth is that they do not buy your products. The opinions that really count are from those people who buy your products and services.

Assessing Development Level

How do you assess your organization's development level? First you will want to determine employees' functioning capabilities and just how much direction you will need to give them. The key questions to ask are:

- Can they solve problems on their own, and do they have good judgment?
- Are they highly energized and motivated?
- Do they work well together?

The answer to the questions will determine the management style you will need to adopt in this environment. In a turnaround situation, you will not find an organization where you can answer yes to all three questions above. In most cases, the answer is no to all three above. If it were yes, rarely would a business find itself in the kind of shape that requires a turnaround.

You need to lead your organization in a participative manner with a high level of employee involvement, but you must manage people in the manner needed to achieve results. You must know when you are leading and when you are managing. There is a difference. For example, managing people involves setting objectives and tracking results. Leading people involves such things as developing mission statements and creating a vision for your business. You must do both. You must not rely solely on one method.

If you have a young, inexperienced but energetic manager, you certainly want to motivate that person by involving him or her in creating a vision for the business. You will also want to manage that person by giving specific directions, guidelines, timetables, and expectations for results. You will want to follow up regularly and monitor progress, offering suggestions and feedback — in other words, coaching and mentoring.

You will also have to evaluate the competency of your key people. This will usually take about six months. You do not have more time than that. You have to make a decision on your key people within six months or less.

Assessing the competency of your staff will take a while. Avoid the mistake of jumping to conclusions based upon initial impressions. There will always be those in an organization who can "talk the talk" but are unable to do as they speak. Often, a glib response can be misinterpreted.

Remember that just as you are evaluating your staff, they are evaluating you as well. What you say and how you interact with them at this critical initial juncture will set the tone for the duration of the turnaround.

What State Information?

The next most critical area to pay attention to is the state of the information reporting system. This encompasses both the financial and the operational reporting systems. In many cases, problems with the information system are what got the company into dire straits in the first place. It's hard to navigate the ship if the compass and radar aren't working!

Evaluating the reliability of the system is tricky. Sometimes it takes an expert in information systems or a CPA to spot the difficulties. Before you hire a high-priced consultant, though, do some of your own investigating.

The first place to start is with the financial reporting system. You don't have to be a CPA to figure out if the numbers are wacky. The easiest way to test the integrity of the financial reporting system is to have a meeting with the financial staff. Look at an interim financial statement (not a year-end one, which probably has been adjusted and finely tuned). Just look at it and then compare it to a year-end financial. Is there a well-designed balance sheet and income statement? Does it include a set of notes? Is there a cash flow analysis? If these basics are missing, you know you have a problem in accounting.

Even the most beautiful financials can be full of baloney. Without doing some real number crunching, it is often hard to find out what's happening. There are a few tricks, though, to identifying financials that aren't up to par. The best way is to start from the balance sheet. Start with cash. That's an easy one to examine. Have the accounting staff show you the bank reconciliation. Is it easy to figure out? Are there a lot of funny adjustments? (Yellow light goes on!) Does the reconciled amount on the bank reconciliation equal the amount on the balance sheet? (If not, the sirens and red lights should be going off.)

Walk on down the balance sheet. Ask for supporting analyses to each of the figures. The accounts receivable should agree with an aging of amounts owed. The inventory should agree with an analysis of inventory. The prepaid expenses should be equal to a worksheet calculating them. You shouldn't have to be a CPA to understand these figures. If you encounter any amount which either can't be explained or isn't supported by a logical analysis, you have stumbled on a potential dumping ground used to "balance the books," hide losses, or squirrel away things that aren't understood.

Do the same thing with the accounts payable, the notes payable, and the other liabilities. You should pay particular attention to inter-company liabilities (what one division owes another). The list should be broken down by division and not lumped together. Right there, in the middle of the meeting, call a few of the other divisions and ask what their balance sheets show. If your company shows a $40,000 liability, it should be a $40,000 receivable on someone's balance sheet. If not, you have a big problem.

Each and every number on the balance sheet should be supported with a detailed analysis, which you should be able to understand. Remember that the accounting staff is likely to be intimidated and may try and "snow" you with complex and confusing analyses. Don't buy it. If you can't fully understand it, then the analyses aren't any good. If you can't verify it, then the analysis is bogus.

Assuming you get down to the end of the balance sheet without many problems, it's time to go on to the income statement. Here is where operational information and accounting information often clash. Accountants record sales and expenses based on a set of rules that are independently established. Internal accounting sometimes varies from this. What you want to see from your accounting department are financials that are as close to the "generally accepted accounting principles" as possible.

Look at the way revenues are reported. If all sales are lumped into one figure, you are flying blind. If there is only one sales figure, ask whether a product line sales report is available. Ask if a sales-by-location report is available and if a booked sales and shipped sales report is available. Ask if a backlog report is available. If they aren't available, find out why. Begin to ask serious questions.

If you have a decent breakdown of sales to evaluate how operations are going, then take them and see if the total agrees to the amount shown on the interim financial statement. If they don't, you are due an explanation — and that should be interesting. Since they all should come from the same information, they ought to be the same. Any differences point to a serious flaw in the financial system.

Now look at the cost of goods sold section of the income statement. Here is another area that requires careful scrutiny. How is cost of goods sold determined? Since the cost of goods sold depends upon getting a good handle on inventory figures, spend some time focusing on how those are determined on an interim basis. You will probably get a decent-sounding explanation. The proof is in the pudding, however.

Ask about any year-end adjustments to correct the interim methods. If you find out that the accountants had to make massive adjustments at the end of the year to adjust the inventory to actual, you know that the misstatements arose from those interim "assumptions," and as a result, the figures you are looking at for gross margin and cost of goods sold on interim financials are probably useless. It is difficult to drive from Chicago to Los Angeles if the map keeps sending you east and then you find out that you are in Philadelphia and have to backtrack.

The area of cost accounting is one that some accountants spend their lives figuring out. It is unlikely that you will be able to fully understand it unless you have taken courses in it. On the other hand, it is vitally important. The areas that must be understood include:

- How is an overhead rate (or burden) calculated? How is it applied?

- Are "standard costs" used, and if so, are there large adjustments to actual costs?

- How is inventory priced? Is LIFO or FIFO used?

- How is the labor applied to the inventory?

- How is the ending inventory quantity determined?

It is way beyond the scope of this book to teach cost accounting. If you don't have a good cost accountant, your company is in serious trouble. One of the primary areas of concentration in your turnaround is to fully understand the cost accounting system. You must determine that:

- All costs are being captured and properly recorded.

- Production costs and overhead costs are being identified and associated with the physical goods.

- Overhead burden (or application rates) are being accurately calculated.

- The holding and inventory costs are being isolated.

- The physical inventory controls are sufficient.

- The system is running smoothly and efficiently.

It may be worth the cost to hire a good CPA firm to look at the costing system if you suspect any problems. Understanding the costs associated with various products is essential to determining pricing and profitability. If you're losing money on one product but don't know it, you may compound your problems when trying to do a fix.

Lastly, it is essential that the accounting system give reasonable accountability of the overhead and month-to-month costs. If you are going to reduce costs, you must understand where they are coming from and what they are. Ask questions. See if the accounting staff has the capacity to print reports that describe the composition of various expense accounts. They should be able to produce them quickly and without much manual analysis work.

Look over the statements for the presence of large "miscellaneous" or "other" expense accounts that constitute dumping grounds for all kinds of expenses. These are tar pits that could hide expenses that should be in other areas.

Finally, look at the timeliness of the financials. If it is April and accounting is still working on January financials, you have a big problem. You should be able to get a month-end financial by the 15th to the 20th of the next month.

Strategic Information

Accountants sometimes think that the financial reporting is all that management needs to run the business. Some managers think that financial reporting is irrelevant to the operations. The truth is that both financial and operational reporting systems are important components of the "central nervous system" of a company.

Before you get too far into the rescue of a company, be sure that you assess the internal operational reporting systems. If they are not working properly, no matter how hard you work, a disaster is unavoidable.

What constitutes the operational reporting? Each company and each industry has different systems, but broadly speaking, an operational reporting system is designed to furnish management with the status of the operations. Some of the common elements include:

- Labor hours and productivity
- Overtime hours and costs
- Burden rates
- Overhead application statistics
- Shop rates (overhead application rate)
- Production levels (units, dollars)
- Production efficiency (as a percent of optimum)
- Production cycle times/Throughput
- Defects/Warranty work
- Inventory levels, aging, and turnover
- Inventory handling efficiency (as percent of optimum)
- Shop utilization/Equipment utilization
- Departmental loads, productivity, and efficiency
- Paperwork processing efficiency
- Sales cycle speed/Turnover
- Sales prospects
- Sales conversion rates (prospects to customers)
- Customer retention/Reorder statistics
- Advance sales bookings
- Prospective sales
- Prospective production costs
- On-time statistics
- Sales activity (appointments, mailings, etc.)
- Advertising reach, pull, and cost per sale
- Marketing efficiency (cost per sale)
- Various departmental statistics such as:
    - Number of invoices generated/Payables
    - Invoices processed/Paychecks processed
    - Warranty claims handled
    - Inbound/Outbound telephone calls
    - Employee applicants
    - Sick days/Vacation days analysis
    - Rework statistics

Many of these statistics are important as part of an information processing and decision-making system. Some of the statistics may be computer generated; others may come as the result of a little scrap of paper kept on someone's desk. The entirety of the system must be integrated to provide management with as true a picture as possible regarding the status of operations.

One of your first priorities as part of an overall assessment should be to graph out the way in which information flows from the various parts of the company up to the decision-making levels. There should be effective systems to monitor:

- Staffing (how many employees are necessary and in what capacities)
- Employee feedback and satisfaction
- Staff development and education
- Inventory of raw materials and finished products
- Production efficiency
- Collection of receivables
- Payment of liabilities
- Overhead costs
- Management of cash resources (inflows and outflows)
- Production deadlines
- Quality control /Warranty costs/Rework costs
- Marketing efficiency and effectiveness
- Labor efficiency and staffing levels
- Advance bookings and sales prospects (for pro-duction planning)
- Customer feedback and satisfaction
- Public relations programs

Many times, you will find that the causes of the company's problems lie squarely in the circle of reporting systems. Erroneous or out-of-date information led to erroneous decisions.

How do you determine whether the reporting systems are working? It is extremely difficult because, unlike accounting, there are often few checks and balances to promote accuracy and self-identify errors. The best approach is to dig. Start with the reports that are generated. Where did they come from? Who generated them? How were they checked or verified? Follow the chain of data back to the origination point. Then ask yourself, "What could possibly go wrong here?"

Another clever way to figure out whether things are working right is to take reports from past periods and correlate them with financial results and other statistics. For example, the production reports could be reconciled with inventory reports. Obviously if you are producing 1000 widgets a day and your inventory reports show a constant inventory, but you are only selling 500 a day, something is terribly wrong. It's either the report or the process.

Try to create a listing of each report, where it comes from, what it is used for, and what it contains. Look for duplication, spurious data, and potential for error. See if there are ways in which the data can be self-checking or reconciled to known figures at periodic points. This process is not simple, and it will be all the more difficult because the chances are that the people you will work with in this investigation will feel threatened by your questioning of their traditional reporting process.

Don't be surprised if you find gaping holes in the information reporting systems. It is not unusual for a company that is in trouble to have been blindsided because they didn't have the proper information reporting systems in place. Less common, but still prevalent, is a system, the hand-me-down of some informal procedure started eons ago, in which irrelevant information is gathered, processed, and put into a report which finds its home in some file, never utilized. Staff people have a propensity to follow tradition blindly, and operations people often fail to question the information they are given.

If you ascertain that the current reporting systems are working correctly, or at least within an acceptable tolerance for error, the next step is to find out how this information is being utilized.

The purpose of information is to tell you how you are doing, where you are going and where you have been (past, present, and future). You've assessed whether the present information is correct, now the task is to determine whether the information will allow a reasonable interpretation of where the company is going.

The process of using historical information to project the future is as much an art as it is a science. Your company probably got into trouble in part because it was unable to make the leap from the present to get a realistic forecast of the future. Many companies fail to do any kind of in-depth forecasting; in some situations the prior year's plan is dragged out, the numbers changed by some arbitrary percent, and a plan is born.

In the best companies, the planning process is an ongoing function. It begins with an assessment of how prior plans are being actualized, an analysis of the causes of the differences, and a steady accumulation of signals as to where the future is headed. Intelligence gathering includes competitors, vendors, customers, industry statistics, and overall economic indicators. Clues are sought out from every corner, from every department, and on every level. The process is company-wide and ongoing. As a result, the entire company is involved in assessment, measurement, projection, and revision. The plan becomes a means of management, assessment, and direction.

Right up front get a good feeling for the type of planning that is taking place, at what levels and with what validity. If you are to chart your company to success, it is imperative that you have a good plan. The planning process is one area that you cannot overlook.

Avoid the temptation to jump in and put out immediate fires. You can easily be consumed by the day to day and never get to the important stuff. Remember that before any general goes into battle, they have a battle plan, with contingencies and "Plan B" and "Plan C." You have to be ready with the same kind of planning.

Talking to Costumers

The next thing you must do while assessing your key managers and supervisors is to talk to your customers. You find out what is wrong and how to improve by asking customers. Most of them will tell you. So go talk to the 20% of customers that make up 80% of your sales. Don't even try to develop a vision for your business until you know what the needs of your key customers are.

Preparing a vision statement before you know your customer's needs is like designing a ship without knowing how it will be utilized. Will it be an oil tanker or a cruise ship? If you don't know, your design is bound to be wrong.

The information you need from your customers is not complicated. It can be straightforward. It is normally limited to the following categories:

- Pricing
- Quality
- Service
- Product performance (for example: speed, productivity, etc.)

The information you need from your customers must be obtained face to face. Why? The sad truth is that some customers will intentionally mislead you. It is almost impossible to tell over the phone because you are not getting any visual feedback.

I walked into a customer's office in the New York City area with my sales rep. It was a huge room, about 100 feet by 100 feet. He had an old, steel case desk, ratty chair, and linoleum on the floor. I didn't have to be a rocket scientist to figure out this guy wasn't making mega bucks. I asked him how we were doing for his company. He answered that our prices were too high, our deliveries were always late, and our quality was poor. I smiled, looked him in the eye and said, "Had I known we were doing that well I wouldn't have asked!" We both laughed and got down to the nitty gritty. The benefit of meeting in person was that I gained a better understanding of the customer's needs by viewing his position. Obviously, he was on a tight budget, and this concern shaped his opinion of our performance. If we were going to improve, we had to be sensitive to the customer's situation, which was something I probably would not have learned over the phone.

Always pick your sales rep's brain before going in to speak to a customer. It will not only prepare you but will also help you evaluate how much your rep really knows about what is going on with the account after listening to the customer's version.

It is beneficial to travel with your sales reps to key accounts early in the process. You will not only obtain feedback from your customers, but it will also allow you to assess your sales reps' abilities. My experience is that most companies that are failing by and large have less than sterling sales reps. There are always exceptions, and I have been blessed with some very good ones in my career. Get out there early and get out there often.

One very important point—**you must take written notes**. It never ceased to amaze me how many experienced salespeople never take notes while in the customer's office. It turned out that my biggest customer in one of my businesses evaluated a salesperson by their written note taking in his office.

Once you determine the root causes of your problems in the marketplace, you must marshal your resources to address it. This is when a vision statement must be prepared. For example, if your prices are too high, are you going to be the premier supplier of high-quality goods or compete with developing countries on wages?

Summary

Assessing the management style needed, laying the foundation we talked about earlier, and assessing the needs of your customers will give you plenty to do. This is how you get a business back on its feet. You will be addressing the right stuff, and you will be doing it in an effective manner—a pretty good combination. If that is all you have to do, you should have this puppy turned around in no time, right? If you think that is all you have to do, you are in for a rude awakening. Getting those things right, however, is a good start.

So what else is involved in a turnaround? Plenty! In order to accomplish the things necessary to fix a business, you must do it through people. While you can influence people, you can only reasonably expect to fundamentally change about 10% of them. Now remember, you are *not* trying to just tweak your business, you are trying to *transform* it. How can you do this if only 10% of the people can be fundamentally changed? This is the subject of our next chapter.

Chapter Four
Workbook

- Have you assessed the functioning capabilities of each of your key managers? If so, how do they stack up?

Manager Assessment:

- Manager A:

  _____

  _____

  _____

- Manager B:

  _____

  _____

  _____

- Manager C:

  _____

  _____

  _____

- Manager D:

  _____

  _____

  _____

- Manager E:

  _____

  _____

  _____

- What management style do you need to use with each of your key managers?

    - Manager A:

      _____

      _____

    - Manager B:

      _____

      _____

    - Manager C:

      _____

      _____

    - Manager D:

      _____

      _____

    - Manager E:

      _____

      _____

- What key issues have your customers indicated to you that must be improved?

  _____

  _____

  _____

  _____

  _____

- Do you have a clear idea of the issues in the market-place as well as the personnel issues that must be addressed? If so, what are they?

Marketplace Issues:

_____

_____

_____

_____

_____

Personnel Issues:

_____

_____

_____

_____

_____

CHAPTER FIVE

THE TRUE ART OF TURNAROUND

As I said earlier, you cannot achieve a turnaround by yourself. You need help, and you need good help. If you can only fundamentally change about 10% of the organization, how can you achieve support for new ideas and new ways of operating from people who cannot fundamentally change? Good question! This is where the art of leading comes into play. It can be done, but it is not easy. There are some tried and true ways that have enabled me to do it repeatedly. This is what I meant when I said I learned what works and what does not. I also said there are no guarantees.

There is a fine line between being popular and being liked. If you are going to turn a business around, you cannot be popular. You cannot, however, be disliked and gain the following necessary to energize a group to work effectively toward common goals.

The true art of the turnaround then is to gain a broad base of support from the organization while transforming it. The transformation will partially consist of replacing team members who cannot achieve the results you need, energizing the remaining members to a high level of commitment, and getting employees to work together effectively.

You will have to hold people accountable for their results and performance. Some employees will resent this. They will stab you in the back while smiling at you and pretending to be team members. Here is my rule: **Don't judge people by what they say or even just by what they do. The best way to assess commitment is to judge them by what they don't do.** For example, do they actively participate at team meetings? Do they bring information to you and proactively make suggestions? Do they give you updates on what is happening? Do they hold their people accountable for performance?

The sad truth is that most people who are not supporting you will hide their true intentions from you. They will not actively communicate their concerns, fears, and inadequacies. Instead, they will try and block your transformation by not actively supporting it. They will try and block it by bad mouthing it and you to their friends on the floor. They will do this undercover so that you will not see it unless you know to look for certain things. The art of avoiding getting torpedoed is to know the signs. You will not get black and white evidence. You must develop relationships with those who will share what is really going on with you. If you do not, you will probably miss it because you will be too busy to catch everything.

You will need to nurture the relationships of those key employees who have the talent and ability to help your organization. You must, as Stephen Covey says, make regular deposits in their emotional bank accounts. You see, even these people will have to be held accountable for their performance. They may only want to work 40 hours a week. They may not want to address performance issues of the people who work for them. The list is endless. If you confront their behavior and do not have prior emotional deposits, you will lose them and they will secretly withdraw their support even if you are 100% correct.

Gaining the support of the organization is not about being right; it is about appealing to people's emotional needs for job security, attention, support, direction, and recognition. It is about earning their trust. If you think you will gain their support because of the nobility of the cause, forget it! If you think you can gain their commitment from just challenging and developing them, forget it. The fact is that most people will resent your efforts to develop them, regardless of how constructively and politely you do it, unless you first earn their trust. You must make at least two emotional deposits (positive reinforcement) for every withdrawal (constructive criticism). The deposits must be honest and not fabricated. If not, it will backfire and make things worse.

For you to achieve real, fundamental change, your organization must embrace or buy into the need for change and your methods. So how do you convert them to that viewpoint? There are no magic formulas. There are several things I have done repeatedly, however, which have worked.

- I was highly visible on the plant floor and talked to people, not just about work but really getting to know them.

- I kept workers well informed, not just through the bulletin boards but also with monthly information-sharing meetings. I always left time at the end for questions and answers. I took some real heat during these Q & A sessions, but I never flinched. I never stopped spreading the word.

- I actively asked for people's ideas and suggestions. More importantly, we implemented them whenever possible. You must be willing to listen. More importantly, you must be willing to act.

- I personally trained my supervisors and managers in supervisory skills. They addressed issues on the floor, but they always treated people with dignity and respect. They treated people consistently and fairly without favoritism.

- I personally gave people facts and information to support the need for changes we were championing. We worked hard at selling change, not dictating it. We never used fear and intimidation.

Another key thing you must do is to allow the key players, usually your direct reports, to participate in developing strategies, new policies, practices, and procedures. You must be able to manage in a participative style so that they can actually develop the changes you are trying to implement.

So this then is the art of leadership. You must hold people accountable for results and improve their behaviors while getting them to support you. The level of difficulty surrounding this task will depend upon the organization's perception of their plight. If, for example, they feel that they are doing well and that they are managing the business effectively, then getting their support for change will be very difficult and the fallout rate will be much higher.

If, on the other hand, they believe they are in big trouble, then getting their honest support will still not be easy, just easier than it could be under different circumstances. There are a couple of crucial ways to gain the critical base of broad support. One way is to create a sense of urgency. Where there is smoke, there is fire. You must actively preach that if we do not change, we won't get different results. If we do not get different results, we don't get to continue to play the game. The more they believe that they are in serious trouble, the more likely you are to gain support.

However, if you are following this strategy, you must also be careful not to scare off your good people. You must be optimistic about being able to fix the problems and enthusiastic about success. You cannot just spread doom and gloom. The objective is to energize them, not demoralize them.

You must actively work to achieve the participation of your leadership team in the design and implementation of the necessary changes. If the key players are not allowed to participate, then why do you think they will actively support it? They must have ownership of it. This will help keep their level of motivation high because they have a personal invested interest in the project.

Creating a sense of both urgency and ownership will improve your chances of transforming the organization.

Remember, to successfully turn around a failing business, you must transform it, not merely tweak it. Achieving a sense of both urgency and ownership for employees is key.

To make emotional deposits in your top players bank accounts means spending a great deal of time with people. How can you do this and turn the business around, too? The truth is you cannot do it in a 40-hour workweek. It takes an enormous amount of energy and dedication. With Rome burning, the temptation is to "put out the fires." The problem is that there will be so many fires that it will consume all of your time. You have to make time to get to know your key people. Knowing your people means more than just saying good morning to them. It means being there for them in times of need. It means coaching and mentoring them. It means taking a sincere interest in them and developing them.

Yes, they are paying you to improve the bottom line, and you have to deliver. If that is all you do, however, you are missing a golden opportunity. The opportunity is to also accomplish something that will be truly meaningful to you. Sure turning a business around is meaningful, but I am not talking about dollars and cents here. I am talking about the intangibles, the stuff that fulfills your basic beliefs.

In my particular case, developing people gives me a high level of satisfaction and fulfillment. This feeling comes from seeing them grow and become more competent and more capable. As they grow and develop, they become more confident and feel better about themselves. You see, turning around an organization isn't just about dollars and cents. You must also make a group of dejected, demoralized people feel like winners again.

Seeing people blossom and take off is a thing of beauty. It gives me tremendous pleasure as well as fulfills a need I have to help people become the best they can be. Not only does it help me emotionally, but I also learn a lot in the process. Know what it is that fulfills you and satisfy it while you are turning the business around. You will most likely not get much kudos from your bosses, and it is important that your work itself bring about its own kind of reward.

Summary

Your satisfaction must come from within and be self-sustained. If you expect to get it externally, you will be disappointed. Knowing you made a difference to the survival of a business is tremendously self-satisfying. Knowing you helped take people to the next level is priceless. You must have their help to achieve the turnaround. If they can honestly see that you care about them, and you make regular deposits in the emotional bank account, they will be more tolerant of your expectations and constructive criticisms for results and good performance. It does not guarantee that you will be popular. It does mean, however, that most decent people will support you, even if most of them resent being held accountable for their results and performance. This is about the best that you can realistically hope for in a turnaround situation.

Chapter Five
Workbook

- Do you feel as though you have the commitment of your key managers? What criteria will you use in order to accurately assess their commitment? If you do not have the commitment of a key manager, how do you plan to address it with that manager?

_____

_____

_____

_____

_____

- How do you plan to achieve the support of your organization in order to transform your business?   How do you gauge this support?

_____

_____

_____

_____

- What are the three key things you must accomplish in order to successfully engineer a turnaround?

_____

_____

_____

- How do you plan to go about creating a sense of ownership and urgency in order to transform the organization?

_____

_____

_____

_____

_____

CHAPTER SIX

BUILDING THE LEADERSHIP TEAM

To gain the broad base of support from the organization, you must first gain it from your own leadership team—that is, your direct reports. If they aren't solidly behind you, you haven't got a chance. That does not mean that you will always have smooth sailing and that there will not be any disagreements. It does mean that your team will have an established process for dealing with issues.

To be able to turn a business around, you must have a solid, cohesive team that gives you 100% support. Besides having good talent, they must work together well and be committed. Here is a basic truth: If they are going to be able to function in this manner, *you* must take reponsibility for developing them in order to reach this level.

Don't think that this will happen automatically. It may, but in most cases it does not. Remember, you only have one year, so don't wait—start immediately. Spend a huge amount of time, effort, and money building teams with your direct reports. The best way I know of is to have a formal team-building program. The following is an outline of the team-building program I have used with many teams.

TEAM BUILDING OBJECTIVES

- To understand the value and benefits of teams and teamwork
- To establish the functioning capabilities to work as a team and hold effective meetings

Suggested Processes	Tools	Outcomes
1. Foundation of team building	• Group discussion: Do we want to be a team? • Team building outline	• Understanding of what a team is
Survival exercise (see Appendix)	• Snow Storm • Facilitator	• Value of team input and consensus
2. Meeting skills training: design questions, roles, and consensus rules	• Facilitator	• Ability to conduct effective meetings • More successful meetings
3. Ground rules of behavior at team meetings	• Brainstorming • Facilitator	• Agreed upon team norms
4. Development of the core team contract	• Candor, brainstorming • Honesty, commitment	• Agreed upon team norms • Written document pledging commitment
5. Team mission statement/Build a vision for your business (chapter 13)	• Documented visioning process • Facilitator	• Written mission/vision statements for the team and the organization
6. One-on-one feedback	• Start/stop exercise • Facilitator	• Improved self-discovery • Bonding

I have done team building with outside facilitators and have been a facilitator myself. Both approaches have been effective. Since most general managers or COOs are not equipped to facilitate team building, you will probably need to obtain an outside facilitator.

There are many different tools to utilize to accomplish team building. Do not just accept the program that the consultant recommends. It must be tailored to your specific needs. You must do formal team building early in the process. Do not wait until you are comfortable with one another. Don't wait until you feel that you have learned the business. Don't wait, period! You must do this within the first three months that you are on the job. "Well," you say, "we are losing money, and this will be a cost for which we didn't budget." Trust me when I say you cannot afford not to do it!

You can expect resistance from several potential areas. Corporate or your controller might say you can't afford it. Your team members might say that they are too busy. The list goes on indefinitely. You will probably have to take the bull by the horns, and as the Nike ad said, just do it!

The team building that I am promoting isn't the kind where you play sports or have paintball wars. The team building I am promoting is a process where you build trust. You develop a belief that your group will make decisions as a group and that you can disagree with each other.

Not all decisions can or should be made by the group. Setting pricing, for example, shouldn't be done by the leadership group. Such decisions as setting policies, business strategies, rules and regulations, developing budgets, planning company events and programs, addressing cross-functional issues, and information sharing can and should be done as a group.

1. Foundation of Team Building

In order to build a team, you must have a well-defined process. This is your starting point on the road toward effective teams. In order to create a team, there are fundamentals that your group must understand. Every team should outline and discuss the following key points as a means to beginning the team-building process:

- What is a team?
- What do functioning teams require?
- Why do we want to be a team? What are the positives and negatives of teams?
- What are the expectations of team members?
- What are the expectations of team leadership?
- What kinds of issues, projects, and work will be done by the team?
- What is the mission of the team?
- How will the team operate?

Your team must understand what a team is and what the requirements for a functioning team are. Once these basics are covered in a group discussion, move on to outlining the expectations of team members and leadership. Such discussions solidify the purpose of the team and give people the opportunity to think about why they want to be a team. With this foundation, the group can move on to discussing the kinds of issues on which they will work, the team's mission, and how the team will operate.

If these key issues are not made clear up front and resolved, your team will never reach its peak potential. Therefore, each issue should be discussed and outlined as a team before you attempt to tackle any other issues. To aid the foundation building, see the Appendix for a "survival exercise," which will help with team development.

2. Meeting Skills

In order to have effective meetings that run smoothly, you must focus on the meeting skills of the group. A meeting should not be an arbitrary, unfocused gathering. A meeting can be looked at as a *process*. As such, it is subject to being managed toward greater efficiency and effectiveness through the application of the P.D.R.C. model's concepts (chapter two):

- Purpose
- Direction
- Regulation
- Capability

In order to apply these concepts, certain information about the meeting must be understood by those who are participating. Groups can develop better meeting skills, which will lead to smoother, more effective meetings. First, you must start with the basic foundation. Much of that fundamental information can be developed through the use of preparation and design questions, definition of participant roles and functions, and consensus rules.

Preparation and design questions help to focus the group and outline the specific purpose of the meeting. Answering these questions for each meeting can produce a discussion that helps everyone know the focus and goals of the meeting. Examples of these types of questions include:

- What is the subject of the meeting?
- What value will result from this meeting?
- What results will we produce in this meeting?
- What process(es) will be used in this meeting to exchange and develop ideas?
- What skills, capabilities, or resources will be required in this meeting?

It is important that each member know exactly what is expected of him or her within the context of the meeting. **Roles and functions** should be clearly defined for each member and understood by all. The four main roles that members will have are: discussion leader, scribe or recorder, auditor or process observer, and participant.

The discussion leader helps the group accomplish its task by providing overall leadership. He or she focuses on the process that the group employs and ensures that necessary roles are filled. The leader must also make sure that all participants are clear on the value, results, processes, and capabilities for each task that the group undertakes. Responsible for keeping the group on track and moving forward on schedule, the leader develops common understanding of group norms or ground rules. He or she must see that all participants are allowed to contribute and then test for consensus. Finally, the leader summarizes points and ideas to aid group understanding.

The scribe or recorder helps the group accomplish its task by capturing the product of the group's efforts and making that product visible to the group. This role supports participants in expressing their thoughts clearly and concisely. The scribe's focus is on the products of the group processes. He or she must listen carefully, conceptualize what is said, and record it in a legible, organized way that displays the essential meaning.

The true purpose is really to help the group recognize it's progress rather than precisely document all the words that are said. The scribe may use an e-board or flip chart in order for the group to see what was agreed to and discussed.

The auditor or process observer helps the group accomplish its task by observing and stimulating improvements in the way that the group works together. He or she assesses the capability the group is employing and it's compatibility with the process and product. The scribe observes the group processes with regard to:

- Adherence to norms
- Quality of communications
- Level of participation
- Quality of thought
- Adherence to process
- Focus — content, relationships, and energy

The scribe is also responsible for enforcing the team's meeting rules of behavior and immediately calling out team members on violations. He or she makes appropriate interventions in the form of observations, questions, and process suggestions.

The final role is that of participant. The participant helps accomplish the task by managing his or her own thinking and behavior consistently with the purpose, direction, regulation, and capability required by the task. Participants must support the meeting leader, scribe, and auditor in fulfilling their roles. Participants must share information fully and openly, listen effectively enough to understand the views of others, and assume accountability for the group's completion of its task.

In addition to focusing on the task and meeting individual role responsibilities, members must also follow **consensus rules** when making decisions in order to ensure that the group operates effectively. Consensus rules will aid the flow of discussion and help the group reach an acceptable agreement. The following is a discussion of the main consensus rules that I have found effective.

Members should avoid arguing their own position. Any position should be presented as lucidly and logically as possible, but members should be sensitive to and seriously consider the reactions of the group in any subsequent presentations of the same point. They should avoid win-lose stalemates in the discussion of opinions. The notion that someone must win and someone must lose should be discarded. When impasses do occur, the group should look for the next most acceptable alternative for all the parties involved.

Members should avoid changing their mind for the sole purpose of avoiding conflict and reaching agreement and harmony. They must withstand pressures that have no objective or logically sound functions. The group should avoid conflict-reducing techniques such as the majority vote, averaging, bargaining, coin flipping, trading out, and the like. Differences of opinion should be treated as indicative of an incomplete sharing of relevant information on someone's part or as related to task issues, emotional data, or "gut level" intuitions.

Differences of opinion should be viewed as natural and helpful rather than as a hindrance in decision making. Generally, the more ideas that are expressed, the greater the likelihood of conflict will be but the richer the array of resources will be. The group should view the initial agreement as suspect and explore the reasons underlying apparent agreements. The group should make sure that people have arrived at the same conclusions for either the same basic reasons or for complementary reasons before incorporating such opinions into the group decision.

Subtle forms of influence and decision modification should be avoided. For example, when a dissenting member finally agrees, the group should not feel that he or she must be "rewarded" by having his or her own way on some subsequent point. Also, the group must be willing to entertain the possibility that they can actually excel at their task. They must avoid "doomsaying" and negative predictions for group potential.

Team members must understand that a consensus must be reached and that no decision is worse than one that is 80% correct. They should also recognize that to reach consensus, it might be necessary to support an action plan or decision that would not have been their first choice but which they can still support. As a result of following these consensus rules, the group should arrive at high-quality decisions that each member actively supports.

Group Effectiveness

There are still a few things to consider in order for the group to perform more effectively. The style of leadership employed is very important. The leadership should be democratic or "participative" so that the interpersonal climate will be relatively free of fear and authority. All members should feel that they share equally in opportunities for influencing decision making. This way, too, there will be opportunity for "alternating" leadership based on relevant expertise and group needs.

Another important element to group effectiveness is the communication patterns that are used. They should be flexible so that all members are able to participate equally and at will. Minority opinions must be encouraged so that they will be voiced. Members should deal openly and honestly with one another. This way there are no "hidden agendas," and personal needs do not impede decisive decision making. Feelings of anger, fear, or doubt can be discussed at the time they are experienced, rather than causing team members to fail to support decisions.

Finally, good problem-solving approaches and decision-making processes must be in place. A cooperative problem-solving approach to conflict and discussion should be employed rather than a competitive win-lose approach. Disagreements can then be viewed as legitimate rather than argumentative and will therefore be encouraged. Individuals will become more receptive to the viewpoint of others. The decision–making process should favor a sharing of responsibility via a respect for individual rights rather than processes that place the responsibility in the hands of a few members. All members should share the burden of successfully accomplishing the necessary task. All members should feel a sense of responsibility for group success.

3. Rules of Meeting Behavior

Besides following a process for conducting a meeting, you should have meeting rules of conduct. The auditor should be charged with observing people's conduct so that they comply with the rules. The auditor should flag violations as they occur and not wait until the meeting is over before addressing violations.

It is critical that each team make up their rules as a team and that the boss not hand them down. Examples of meeting rules of conduct are:

- Demonstrate mutual respect.
- Have an agenda, be on time, and take notes.
- Support each other and a consensus decision 100%.
- Don't dominate the conversation or the meeting.
- Stay focused on the issues at hand.
- Agree to disagree utilizing facts; do not just argue out emotion. Be open and listen to all ideas.
- Maintain complete confidentiality.
- Stay focused on ideas and not on people.
- Stay flexible. Take turns.
- Complete assignments on time unless approved.
- Participation in discussions isn't optional.
- Be cooperative. Have fun!

4. Team Contracts

The team contract is a key element of team building that is often left out of the process. These are examples of team contracts. What is important is that your team develops their own contracts, uses them, and enforces them. The team must reach an agreement as to what behaviors are critical to your team's success. Examples are:

- Be honest with each other.
- Be open-minded.
- Have high standards of work ethic.
- Actively support the right to disagree and promise to respect dissenting opinions.
- Monitor and support each other to achieve success.
- Maintain confidentiality.
- Do not avoid addressing negative comments made in our presence about people in the company.
- Fully commit to our team contract.

An enforcement policy should also be included in your team contract. Without some form of discipline, there becomes less and less incentive to adhere to the rules. This is an example of an enforcement policy:

Enforcement of Team Contracts:

Step 1

Must confront teammate one on one:
- Privately
- Timely
- Allow person time to respond
- If not resolved, both parties must agree to step two

Step 2

Involve another teammate as an impartial mediator. If unresolved, both parties must agree to step three.

Step 3

Team Tribunal
- A group of peers who review the problem and render a judgment

Step 4

Team decision on membership for repeat offenders

A formal enforcement process is the vehicle that allows teams to resolve conflict and continue to function as a team. Without a formal enforcement process of the team contract, teams eventually break down and stop functioning effectively. An enforcement process will allow your team to behave according to the contract members have established for themselves. The team contract is a code of voluntary cooperation.

For a team to be effective, members cannot sit on the sidelines. All team members must become involved. The real essence of a team contract is peer pressure. Hopefully, it replaces backstabbing and blame shifting with cooperative monitoring, support, and reinforcement.

The key to effective team contracts is trust. If teammates trust one another, members are much more likely to accept the constructive criticism from one another. Confronting another teammate who violated the team contract isn't optional; it is mandatory.

I have had several teams develop contracts. Without fail, they take teams to a new level. Most importantly, however, your team will have a defined, written process for dealing with team members who violate the contract. Without a formal, written process to enforce the team contract, it isn't worth the paper on which it is written.

I have had a team take a member to a team tribunal. The violation was about a plant manager badmouthing one of his supervisors openly to a third party. This behavior was repeated numerous times, and the member also started badmouthing other people as well. When I questioned the plant manager, he denied doing it.

In front of the team tribunal, he said he could not remember whether he had done it or not. After his testimony in front of the team tribunal, we excused him and debated the disciplinary action that should be taken. We unanimously concluded that this behavior wasn't new, nor would a disciplinary action be likely to stop it in the future. The team voted unanimously to remove him from the organization.

Sure, I as the general manager had to run it through my boss and HR. After a few weeks of review, our recommendation was upheld, and he was removed. This process sent a strong message, not only to our organization but to our team as well. They suddenly realized how powerful the team and its contract were. It had an immeasurably positive impact on bonding our team together. The message here is that you should not create any team contracts by which you are not willing to live.

5. Mission Statement

Another element of team building, which normally is included in the process, is creating a mission statement for your leadership team. The team needs to develop this statement — they must own it. These statements define and focus the group. Your role is to explain the boundaries. What type of decisions will the team make? How will the team operate? What is your role? Are you still the boss or, during team meetings, are you just a teammate? These issues must be discussed in detail and be clearly understood. You see, it takes an enormous amount of self-confidence as well as trust in your team to "lose control." The truth is that you cannot gain commitment until you lose control.

Here is my rule: **Commitment is much more powerful than control.** Getting the total commitment of your leadership team is absolutely critical to being able to salvage the business. You must possess the character that allows you to be a teammate in team meetings rather than the boss. This takes courage and a deep trust in teams. It is not something you can get out of a book. This is another reason why it is more difficult for younger, inexperienced leaders to be able to turn around businesses.

Mission statements are like three-legged stools. The key legs of the mission statement that must support it are:

- The shareholders

- The customers

- The employees

These are three major components of a business and each must be addressed in your statement. Get one out of balance and the stool will topple. A good mission statement addresses all three camps. A good example of a mission statement from one of my businesses is the following:

> Through synergistic and professional cooperation, we commit to achieving individual and collective goals through the open development and implementation of ideas, teaching and influencing others, and sharing knowledge, which will enhance winning results and create a lasting, successful enterprise, ensuring safe and secure futures.

Another mission statement from one of my businesses looks like this:

> We the management team of XYZ Company will promote the general welfare and help secure the future of our company and people by improving profit, service, and our reputation. We promise to work together effectively by being dedicated to each other's success.

I have also included a vision statement as part of the team-building process. I will talk more about vision statements in section two of this manual. Why include the vision statement as part of the foundation building and as part of the operational changes? Because it really does do both! I will revisit this topic in section two.

6. One-on-One Feedback

Another critical team-building process that is often overlooked is the one-on-one feedback. This is the last drill in the process to go through. This is where each member of the team spends time, one on one, giving honest feedback to each other. One teammate gives the other person two or three things that he or she really appreciates about the person as well as two or three things that could be improved.

There has to be ground rules, however, to successfully accomplish this. The rules are:

- The recipient cannot argue with the giver; he or she can only ask questions for clarification.
- The communicator of the information has to give specific examples and not just generalities.
- The information is given in a caring, polite way (no personal attacks).

This process can really bring a team together. Sure it is uncomfortable. If you as "the boss" do not receive some constructive criticism that comes as a surprise to you, then you can conclude that your team hasn't yet bonded and that they have whitewashed your feedback. On the other hand, if you do get some bad news about yourself, you are ahead of the game because you have something concrete on which to focus and work toward improving.

I never said team building would be easy. It isn't. If it were, there would be many more happy, successful teams. (Remember what I said about courage?)

Summary

Team building is a difficult, time-consuming process. While I am all for building teams on the plant floor, if you expect to turn a business around in one year, you simply don't have time. You can and you must have a solid business leadership team behind you. My experience is that you will have at least one member who cannot function as an effective member of a business leadership team. Be prepared to deal with these members. Don't procrastinate. The person's problem might be competence, teamwork, or it could be constantly violating your team covenants. Whatever the case, you must deal with it fairly and quickly or else you are jeopardizing the future of your business.

Chapter Six
Workbook

- How committed are you to developing a leadership team in order to reach the organization's potential and successfully turn the business around? How important is it to success?

_____

_____

_____

_____

- What kind of formal team-building program are you planning to utilize? Are you utilizing outside help? If not, what experiences do you have that will help you?

_____

_____

_____

_____

- Do you plan to develop team covenants? If not, why not? If so, do you plan to have your team develop the covenants and methods to enforce them?

_____

_____

- Do you plan to use one-on-one feedback? If so, how do you plan to accomplish it?

_____

_____

_____

_____

_____

- How should you go about forming your leadership team's mission statement?

_____

_____

_____

_____

- What are the three legs of a team's mission statement? Write out your mission statement. Does your mission statement have all three legs?

_____

_____

_____

_____

_____

_____

CHAPTER SEVEN

SUPERVISORY TRAINING

Providing good supervisory training for the entire organization is critical to the transformation process. If your managers and supervisors are verbally abusing your people, playing favorites, being dishonest and inconsistent, or simply displaying poor management skills, your organization will never develop good morale much less the high productivity, teamwork, and ownership necessary for results. These are characteristics that your organization must have to set yourself apart from the competition and to ensure survival.

It helps to have good equipment in good condition. In the final analysis, however, it is the people that make a difference. Sure, your business can have patents that are making you successful. This is, however, the exception. Remember that your competition can usually buy comparable equipment and technology to match you. You normally cannot establish a lasting competitive advantage in any industry through equipment. It is how the people use the equipment that counts. Vaughn Beals, former CEO of Harley Davidson, said that their manufacturing used to be the worst in the industry. Oil leaked from every cycle they made. He then said that they transformed the business and accomplished the best tolerances in the industry. They did it with the same old equipment. The secret was to empower their employees — their employees took ownership for the quality of the product. There is no real magic here; they just came to the realization that management was the problem.

In order to create a lasting competitive advantage, not to mention transforming your business, you must manage your people in a participative manner. You must empower them. Empowerment does not mean that you give them a blank check. You must set and define boundaries. Within those boundaries, however, you want people to make as many decisions as possible about how they do their work.

By getting your people actively involved in decision making and problem solving, you will achieve employee ownership of results. Once you achieve that, you have a competitive advantage. You cannot achieve this with dictatorial managers and supervisors.

The beginning step in realizing this goal is to train your managers and supervisors. You cannot scrimp or shortcut this step. Sure, it takes time away from production, but if you are to rescue your business, it is mandatory. Do not settle for a simple seminar or top-down lecture on supervision skills. Go for it: use written material describing the how to's, videos of role playing, and role-playing problems for the class to utilize. People learn by reading, seeing, and doing.

It is also a powerful way to transform your organization. I have run seven different manufacturing plants. None of them had effective supervision when I walked in the door. None of them had managers or supervisors who had received formal supervisory training before I got there.

Of the seven different manufacturing plants, one was a start-up, two were doing reasonably well, and the other four were failing. Do you think this is a coincidence or could there may be a distinct connection? Businesses that do not have good leadership and supervisory management do not have a high probability of success, in a turnaround situation or under normal circumstances.

Invest in your people. Start by developing and training your managers and supervisors in the area of people skills. Your people are your most important resource. Yet, most organizations spend more money maintaining equipment than they spend on developing the people who run that equipment.

Your dilemma will probably be how to do the training. The two available options are to do it yourself or to hire an outside consultant. I was fortunate enough to have the materials, training, and experience to be able to do the training myself. You may be able to do it or you may rely upon a consultant. The point is, this is one area that cannot be overlooked. Despite the fact that you won't have the time or resources, you must commit to it, the sooner the better. Without it, your chances of success are minimal. It may be a coincidence that by effectively employing team building and supervisory training, my teams were four for four in turning around dying businesses, but I doubt it. The training will also give you the opportunity to assess your managers and supervisors close up, away from other distractions.

You must make a crucial judgment. Can your managers and supervisors lead in the way that you need them to lead in order to transform the business? If not, bite the bullet and remove them early and save yourself a lot of grief. They will only frustrate and slow down your transformation. The key is not whether they currently possess the skills because the sad fact is that few do. The question is whether they possess the right character qualities. All the training in the world cannot transform a plow horse into a racehorse. You must assess whether you have the right "breed" for the right job.

Most employers won't let a new employee operate their equipment without weeks or months of training. Yet, most businesses take their employees who have good technical skills and make them supervisors without any formal training. This makes no sense whatsoever. Yet, it is the rule rather than the exception in most manufacturing plants, and we wonder why our manufacturing plants are not making significant gains in productivity! We will talk about this in the next chapter.

Summary

The bottom line is that the people working within your organization are its most valuable resource. In order to keep this asset and maximize your people's productivity, you must be able to manage them effectively. Participative management empowers employees and gives them a role in decisions. Empowerment leads to employee loyalty and high-quality work.

To achieve this, you must be willing to invest in your managers and supervisors. They must be able to lead workers for a turnaround to be successful, and chances are that few will actually possess these skills from the start. Training is a difficult task to face when you have little amounts of time and money upon which to draw. However, it will be a crucial element of a turnaround's success.

Chapter Seven
Workbook

- What is the most important resource that your business has? Why is it the most important?

_____

_____

_____

- Why is giving managers and supervisors good training extremely important?

_____

_____

_____

_____

_____

- What kind of supervisory style will you and your managers and supervisors need to transform your business?

_____

_____

_____

_____

CHAPTER EIGHT

EMPLOYEE INVOLVEMENT

There are many ways to get your employees involved, and there are various levels of employee involvement. The most popular method, and the hardest to achieve, is by using teams. If you work for an automotive company or some larger established corporations, chances are that you have already had some experience with teams.

If you are not that fortunate, however, you will be faced with starting them yourself. The truth is that most companies, Fortune 500 companies included, have not developed effective processes to implement and train teams. Most of them also have not spent the money to develop supervisors. Most supervisors are put in their positions because of:

- Their technical knowledge
- Their personal relationship with someone in management, usually the plant manager
- Their seniority

You will probably be faced with supervisors who are dictatorial and behave primarily like babysitters. They are rarely held accountable for results, and they have no skills in holding their people responsible for their performance. These supervisors will be clueless about team concepts. They will probably resist the idea or any idea that threatens the status quo.

There will be other barriers to forming teams. Not having the resources, time, or money is only the beginning. In most cases, you will lack support from the upper management. However, you must do it regardless of the obstacles. Do not think that the team process will be done overnight, however. This task normally cannot be done effectively in the first year. Why? Well, first you must train your supervisors and managers and then assess how well they function.

Since you will want to do your team building with your leadership team first, the supervisory training comes next and then the assessment period. That pretty much takes care of your first year. However, expect that some or all of your supervisors will not be able to successfully make the transition. You have to be prepared to remove them. You can either replace them or run teams without supervisors. My current business had to do the latter. It is not easy, but it is sure more effective than having incompetent supervisors.

Most old-school supervisors will resist taking on more responsibility, having to discipline their people, having to give bad performance appraisals to their buddies, and being held accountable for their results. Their resistance will take the form of guerrilla warfare. It will be fought under cover and will not be directly observable. In a later chapter, we will talk more about accountability on the manufacturing floor.

If you are going to create teams on the manufacturing floor, do not make the mistake of thinking that you have created effective teams if all you do is simply call team meetings and give people t-shirts. Creating manufacturing teams takes *a lot* of time and effort.

First, you must spend time deciding what kind of teams you want and how many. This step is usually overlooked or only given cursory attention. The next step is to select candidates for team leaders and then assess your candidates. The assessment should be done professionally by outside psychologists.

The key criteria that I recommend utilizing to select team leaders are:

- A willingness to do the job duties
- How closely their behavior profile matches the desired profile
- Comprehensive technical skills and knowledge to maximize quantity and quality
- Interpersonal skills

The reason I suggest using an outside psychologist is simple. They have the experience, the tools, and the objectivity to give the process a better chance.

The next step is to devise team guidelines as to how to function and what things you want them to attack. If you do not, they are liable to come up with either a huge list of maintenance items, which they aren't responsible for, or they will offer suggestions that have nothing to do with improved productivity or quality, such as painting the lunchrooms and bathrooms. Don't get me wrong, I strongly believe in having clean restrooms, but that isn't the type of objective on which teams should be principally focused.

If you spend the time up front doing the organizational designing, training, leader selection, and giving guidelines and boundaries, you will be way ahead of most organizations that try to implement teams. There are no guarantees, but you will increase your odds of success tremendously.

Another way of gaining employee involvement is through active participation in various committees such as cost-reduction projects, safety, quality, product development, United Way, company picnics, Christmas parties, etc. The participation in these committees should not be in lieu of teams; they should complement teams. I have had tremendous success in forming committees to write rules of conduct for the entire plant.

However you choose to implement employee involvement, you must listen to your people. Once you let the genie out of the bottle, you must be prepared to accept its power and influence. While you cannot let your people run the business for you, you must listen to their suggestions. Again, you must set boundaries and guidelines. However, if every idea they make gets turned down, they will stop offering suggestions and view the entire process as a time-wasting charade. If you do not listen to your people, they will quickly become demoralized, and you will have achieved the worst kind of negative environment.

While healthy businesses have the time and financial buffer to recover from this, failing ones do not. You cannot afford to make a catastrophic mistake. Here is a key point: A lot of teams fail because the team members become disenchanted due to their perception that management isn't listening to their suggestions. You had better *listen* or your teams will fail, too.

Summary

Look at manufacturing floor teams as a long-term investment and certainly not a quick fix. Do not try and fix the business through manufacturing floor teams and expect to achieve huge gains within twelve months. You will achieve huge gains, but it is highly unlikely that you can do it in the time frame with which you are faced.

If you have a 12-month time frame, start the process with key committees and put your resources into team building with the leadership team. Focus on you supervisors' people skills training and an effective assessment and selection of your team leaders. This way you can be making operational progress while still laying a foundation for the future.

Chapter Eight
Workbook

- What will probably be the single biggest impediment to forming your manufacturing teams and why?

_____

_____

_____

_____

_____

- What is the most important thing you must do in order to make employee involvement work?

_____

_____

_____

_____

_____

- How soon should you expect to be able to start achieving significant gains from you plant teams?

_____

_____

_____

_____

_____

CHAPTER NINE

SHARING INFORMATION

The Information-Sharing Meeting

If you want your people to trust you and to become involved and take ownership for results, then you must share information with them on a regular basis. I am not talking about putting up memos on bulletin boards (not that I'm against that), but rather, I recommend face-to-face meetings every four to six weeks.

I have shared information with employees about almost everything going on in the business. It is a way to communicate significant changes that impact the factory floor. In my current business, I have addressed the following issues with workers within a 12-month period:

- A layoff of 20% of the work force
- Going to a four shift, seven-day work week
- Forming two separate teams across the plant and eliminating the supervisory positions

In addition to the major issues mentioned above, I share our financial results, our pending business, what we are doing to reduce costs on our materials, new technical developments, quality issues, safety, new programs, etc. The list is endless. I always close the meeting by taking questions from the floor. I explain that I will take questions, but if they have complaints, they must see me one on one. You don't want a big meeting to turn into an uncontrolled grievance session.

I hold these meeting with all three shifts. How do I do that? I do it by getting up in the middle of the night and going in to work. It is crucial that you are available to all workers, and it is critical that you be open and honest. If someone asks you about something confidential, such as a pending acquisition, you can respond that you are not at liberty to discuss that issue. It is better to not say anything than to appear as though you are being evasive.

The monthly information-sharing meeting is also a way to gain credibility with your people. By telling them openly and honestly what is going on, you are building credibility. Let's face it; you need the ideas of your troops in order to improve your operation. By gaining their respect, you can gain their trust and willingness to work with you a lot faster, and people will be more likely to share their opinions with you.

It is important that you try to get to know each employee on a first-name basis. This will be difficult because a great deal of the time must be spent fighting the organization's fires. You will feel like you do not have enough time for chitchat and rightfully so. However, you must make the effort to be available for employees and meeting with them once a month will at least give you the chance to talk to all of them. Remember, people are the organization's most valuable asset, and it is up to you to see that they are not neglected.

Bring in other speakers, be it your sales manager, plant manager, etc. Let the troops see how united your team is. Let them see how your team enjoys being together. Use overheads, graphs, hard data, pictures, etc. Put time and effort into the presentation, just as you would for your boss. It will pay huge dividends.

The Eatin' Meetin'

In each of the organizations I have managed, there have been varying levels of commitment and competence. In order to bring your management team together, you will need to meet and meet often.

In a turnaround situation, your leadership team will have more to do than they think they have time for

because they will be so busy. Since their level of commitment will not be uniform, several team members will
complain that they cannot get their work done because
they have to attend too many meetings.

An effective way to address this complaint is the
"eatin' meetin'." I have planned a lot of my meetings from
noon to 2:00 PM. I normally had lunch brought in for the
group. In this way, the employees were only giving up one
hour of their time and not two. In addition, they got a free
lunch.

The complaints stopped immediately. While this may
seem like a pretty juvenile way to deal with the issue, the
truth is that it works. You must address your team's objec-
tions on the level of development that they are at, not the
level of development where you would like for them to be.

The Electronic Blackboard

One of the most effective things I have done consistently in all of my turnaround situations is buy an
electronic blackboard. The electronic blackboard (or
whiteboard) allows you to accurately record anything
written on it. The device looks like a regular whiteboard,
but as you make notes on it, they are captured digitally.
Later, a verbatim copy of the board can be printed out on
8 ½ x 11" paper. They are about $1,600 and are worth
every penny of it. Why, you ask? The reason is that if you
are going to transform your business, you must have the
full participation of your leadership team and supervisors.

An electronic blackboard accomplishes many objectives
for you. It can accurately capture your meeting minutes,
ideas, and action plans and can ensure that people know
who needs to be doing what and when they need to be
doing it. It communicates this information on a timely basis.

I have sat in meetings where issues were discussed
and a vague agreement was reached that so and so would
research something and get back to the group. Well, so

and so either consistently forgets or is too busy to do it, and since there isn't a written record, it is forgotten.

In a nutshell, so many failing businesses are failing because of vaguely defined action plans and a lack of documentation and communication as to what was agreed. The electronic board not only captures what is being said, it lets the entire group see what is being agreed to at the time. It allows the group to make changes on the fly. It allows the group to understand what is being agreed to, who will do it, and when it is to be done. Copies can be made right at the end of the meetings, and everyone walks out with the same information in their folders.

Action Plans

In meetings, a main goal is to create action plans to solve problems or implement new projects. Action plans must be given attention, as they are critical to the success of a proposed venture. How they are designed may affect the outcome. An important item to consider is that your plan has all the critical elements. It is important that your plans be action oriented. Planning without key actions is mere jawboning. When you address a problem, you must have a results-oriented plan of action. The action plan should contain key elements, formatted separately in columns:

- A summary description of the project
- A designated project coordinator who is responsible for the project
- Key objectives or deliverable products or outcomes that need to be accomplished
- Dates by which the objectives will be accomplished
- A specified completion/review date as well as any interim review dates

Most failing businesses do not have effective action plans. They have good ideas, but nothing ever gets done. One of your responsibilities is to make sure that the right things get done quickly. By utilizing an electronic blackboard and holding people accountable, you will quickly find out who is not getting things done. You will need to follow up with these individuals separately, holding one-on-one conversations with them regarding work habits.

Brainstorming

Often, your team must brainstorm an issue or problem. The objective is to get as much participation as possible and to get the creative juices flowing. The purpose is to get as many ideas as possible on the table. Ideas should not be judged or critiqued at this stage. Later, you can address the practicality, relevance, and effectiveness of these thoughts. Here are my rules for brainstorming:

- Have silent preparation of thoughts and ideas (usually ten to fifteen minutes).
- Have a round robin listing of ideas and proposals.
- There is no debate of the proposals during the round robin, participants can only ask questions.
- Ask questions for clarification.
- Debate and discussion happens after the list is completed and everyone is tapped out of ideas.
- People can pass during a round and still come back with a suggestion during later rounds.
- When you are finished, try to group common suggestions together into common themes.
- You will come up with more ideas and suggestions than you can attack at once, so you must prioritize.
- You *can* utilize voting for prioritization.
- You should *never* use voting for decision making, rather a consensus must be sought.

Summary

In order to gain the loyalty, trust, and dedication from workers that you desperately need, they will have to be kept knowledgeable about what is occurring within the organization. You will have to create ways to share valuable information with employees and communicate with them. I have found that monthly meetings with each shift allow me to get information out to the entire organization. This will take extra work on your part but it is time well spent. To get around time restrictions and other obstacles, you may have to become a little creative, like utilizing an eatin' meetin' or an electronic blackboard. Whatever you do, make sure that everyone is getting the information they need.

Part of being a good leader, however, is also being able to listen and let others communicate their ideas. Communication is not just talking to employees but also hearing what they have to say as well. This is especially important to keep in mind during meetings when you may have the tendency, as the boss, to "run the show" and not allow for full participation. Make sure that everyone is allowed the opportunity to participate.

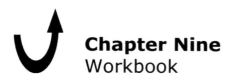

Chapter Nine
Workbook

- Why should you conduct regular information-sharing meetings?

_____

_____

_____

_____

_____

- How can you meet with your off-shift employees?

_____

_____

_____

_____

- Why should you have regular leadership team meetings?

_____

_____

_____

_____

- How should leadership team meetings differ from traditional staff meetings?

_____

_____

_____

_____

_____

- Why should your leadership team meeting *initially* be an eatin' meetin'?

_____

_____

_____

_____

- Since leadership team meetings are team meetings and not staff meetings, what behaviors do *you* need to change in order to facilitate the meeting and not "be the boss " during these meetings?

_____

_____

_____

_____

- What does achieving consensus mean, and how must you as the facilitator behave in order to achieve it? (Hint: You don't vote!)

_____

_____

_____

_____

_____

- What benefits do you realize with an electronic blackboard?

_____

_____

_____

_____

_____

- Why do you need to meet often with your leadership team and supervisors/team leaders?

_____

_____

_____

_____

_____

- What are the key elements of a good action plan?

_____

_____

_____

_____

_____

- Do you have a written format for your action plans? Are you utilizing the forms for all major projects? What are the basics that are constants in your action plans?

_____

_____

_____

_____

_____

- Do you utilize brainstorming frequently in your team meetings? What are the benefits? If not, why not?

_____

_____

_____

_____

_____

- Do you have a formal process to follow when your team brainstorms? What is it? If not, why not?

_____

_____

_____

_____

_____

CHAPTER TEN

REVIEWING THE FOUNDATION

In summary, chapters one through nine detail the key *nonoperational* things I have done to lay the foundation for turning a business around. Of course, there are probably other things that you will have to do; you will need to implement other nonoperational changes and also make operational changes. If you incorporate these nonoperational processes into your game plan, you will greatly increase your odds for success. You must also trust your gut as to what other improvements your business needs.

Even if you make the nonoperational changes described in section one, they will not, *by themselves*, right the ship. You must also be making significant operational changes simultaneously (remember what I said about a high energy level?). You cannot do the nonoperational stuff first and then address the operational stuff; **you don't have enough time.** The truth is, you must do *both* simultaneously and do both quickly.

We talked about having a mission statement, but what about a vision statement and key values and beliefs? I will deal with the vision statement in section two because I believe that it is really part of the operational changes. In regard to values and beliefs, they are important, but they are for the long haul. In a turnaround of one year, they will not be able to help you. You must prioritize and do those things, and only those things, that will help you right the ship the first year.

It is more difficult to give guidelines on the operational changes that you must make. Why? It is because each situation is different. Section two deals with operational changes that I have made in the four businesses that I have successfully turned around. They may not all be applicable to your situation. However, since I have repeatedly had to deal with these issues, I will share them with you.

Section Two

Plugging the Leaks:

Making Operational Changes

CHAPTER ELEVEN

How Do Failing Companies Get Into That Position?

We start off this section of the book asking ourselves this basic, fundamental question: How do failing businesses get into that position? Obviously, there isn't one clear, universal answer. Let me start by saying that many businesses that are doing well are doing so because of circumstance and not because they are well managed. Just look at the multitude of dot-com companies that have tanked. Everyone was looking at potential, and very few investors were able to evaluate management capability.

All too often a business's potential or its results cannot be evaluated separately from management performance. This means that businesses that are doing well may be doing so because of circumstances, such as:

- Good patents
- Being first to the marketplace
- Finding a niche that has not attracted a great deal of serious competition
- Having an exclusive franchise for your products, geography, or the materials you purchase, such as proprietary paper
- New technology
- State of the art production equipment
- Unusually effective marketing
- Fad or fashion

Many successful companies have products or are in hot markets that make them successful. They are making good money, so they *assume* that they are managing their business well. They are being misled by the return on investment (ROI) and return on sales (ROS) results that they are achieving.

Aren't bottom-line results what it's all about? Yes, they are important, but how you are achieving these results is equally as important. If you are earning 30% ROS but don't have any serious competition, does that mean you are managing well? More importantly, what things are your management teams doing to be able to successfully defend your results against a formidable competitor? On the other hand, a business earning 10% ROS in an industry which is saturated with strong competitors might be managed very well. The point is that while well-managed businesses can fail because they can be competing in the wrong industry or with antiquated technology, they also fail because the circumstances of the business change.

The management of a business that has been successful due to circumstances can suddenly find itself facing a crisis for the first time if circumstances change. Dealing with a crisis is much more difficult than dealing with fundamental business issues when you are doing well. If the management team has not developed experience from a solid track record of making tough, unpopular decisions during good financial times, why would anyone believe that they would suddenly be capable of making these tough decisions in a crisis?

What normally happens is that, like the ostrich, they stick their heads in the sand and hope that the storm will pass. They normally try band-aid solutions. Band-aid solutions are ones that normally address the symptoms and not the root causes. Addressing the root cause is very painful and unpopular, and these types of management do not know how to deal with hard decisions.

I have seen a general manager try band-aids for two years in an attempt to address the profitability issues of a plant. He should have closed it up front. He couldn't come to grips with this conclusion because of his personal relationships with the people in the plant. As a result, his entire business suffered as this plant pulled down the profitability achieved by the rest of his plants.

So why does this happen so often in manufacturing businesses? The inescapable answer is the lack of good leadership. Leaders of successful businesses generally get lulled into a false sense of accomplishment and security. They conclude that the success of the business is the result of their skills, not fortunate circumstances. This environment inhibits addressing difficult, core business issues. Their answer is to throw money and capital investment at perceived problems or to create new opportunities.

While companies are willing to invest in new brick and mortar and equipment, rarely do they invest in developing their people in order for them to become effective leaders. The conclusion of most companies achieving good financial results is that they already have good people and good leaders.

Few companies spend the time and money to develop their people. An exception to the rule is a company that spends a significant amount of resources on its training and development. Examples of these companies are General Electric and Procter & Gamble.

While new equipment and technology often help keep businesses competitive, they generally don't make the difference between long-term success and failure. Chances are that competitors can also buy the same equipment. Unless a business has a patent, which can prevent competitors from duplicating their technology, new equipment is generally a short-term advantage. Most businesses don't seem to understand this. Why then do they bank on new equipment to salvage their plight and create a competitive advantage? It is because they don't focus on the real root causes, which would generally be very painful to address.

Here are some examples of painful issues that tend to be avoided:

- Holding people accountable for results and removing ineffective managers, sales reps, supervisors, and hourly plant employees who cannot be developed into effective performers.
- Closing a plant that is no longer competitive from a cost or technology standpoint.
- Correctly assessing that your business does not have a competitive advantage and taking the necessary steps to develop one or exiting the business in a planned manner.
- Changing benefit and retirement packages, the cost of which make your business noncompetitive.
- Establishing good quality practices and procedures.
- Measuring and rewarding your sales people on margin dollars instead of units or dollars of sales.
- Changing the culture of a business (a huge job).
- Segmenting a business into smaller, natural business units and then structuring the organization around these units. Reporting and tracking P&L results by business unit and downsizing units that aren't generating a healthy ROI or ROS.
- Changing out suppliers who aren't providing you with the best value, even though your business has been using them for years.
- Launching new products to grow your business.
- Eliminating R&D projects that are not strategic.
- Holding engineering to cost targets on equipment development programs, which will allow the equipment to be price competitive in the marketplace.
- Significantly reducing cost in your base materials, which requires a cross-functional team effort.

It may seem strange that these things are not addressed. However, I found out that in failing businesses, they tend to be the rule rather than the exception. These unexamined problems are usually the reasons why companies are failing.

Summary

Achieving a successful business can be a dichotomy. You can be successful because of circumstance; you can be successful because you are well managed; and you can be successful because you are well managed and have good circumstances. The trick is knowing into which category you fall. Few management teams really know. Fewer yet can look at themselves and realistically assess their management effectiveness. Why? It is probably because they don't know what they don't know.

Yes, businesses fail all the time because they get blown away by foreign competition, new technology, or lower cost suppliers. I believe most fail, however, because they do not have the kind of leadership that will ensure that if the circumstances will enable them to survive that they will do the painful things necessary to be successful. Yes, well-managed businesses do fail, no question about it. On the other hand, many poorly managed businesses are financially successful.

The challenge facing most American manufacturing management, and management in general, is to realistically assess their position, examine their practices, define their action plans, and do the many difficult things necessary to survive in the long term. It sounds fairly simple. However, since it rarely happens, it is apparently the human element that seems to get in the way of achieving these things. Leaders of businesses are human. **Good leaders are the ones who have the guts and the know-how to do the things necessary to secure the future for their employees and their shareholders**. Good leaders are also capable of accomplishing this rather arduous task in a compassionate and ethical manner.

The second section of this book deals with the actions and practices that I have taken to turn businesses around. These practices address the problem issues that seem to be common to many failing businesses. Don't get me wrong;

you can do all this stuff really well and still fail because of circumstances. If, however, you do these things well, your chances of success are a great deal higher.

Chapter Eleven
Workbook

- In order to effectively transform your business you need to understand why your business is failing. What are the major reasons why your business is failing?

_____

_____

_____

_____

_____

- If your business is successful, what are the major reasons why?

_____

_____

_____

_____

_____

- Have you assessed whether or not you can save this business. If so, why do you believe it is salvageable?

_____

_____

_____

_____

CHAPTER TWELVE
WHERE ELSE DO I GET STARTED?

Where to begin? In the midst of a failing enterprise, there are so many things to do, and they are all screaming for resolution. One of the major strengths you will need is the ability to sort out the critical from the urgent.

Previously, we discussed the importance of understanding the internal systems and organization or how the company functions. This must extend to how the firm is perceived from the outside. To find out what is wrong with the company, you need to know not only how those issues are perceived from within the company but also how outside groups perceive the organization. It is folly to attack only the issues that your people give you or the ones that you hear about from within the company.

The best intelligence about your situation will come from your customers and vendors. You must poll those two sources before making any serious operational plans.

To find out how your customers perceive you, talk to them. Find out why they do business with the company and what could entice them to do more business. Talking to existing customers is a good way to learn about what your company is doing right. It is not always the best way to learn about what the problems are with your organization. To do that, you want to talk to the customers you have lost.

Look back over recent history and have marketing come up with a list of important accounts that you have lost. They are the ones you need to speak to about problems. People will generally be helpful if you ask them, and lost customers are no exception. The objective is not to find out why they stopped doing business but what things at the company could or should have been different so that they could do business. Many of the lost customers will complain about price but remember that price is often just an excuse for other problems. It will take some digging to find out what really happened.

Resist the temptation to delegate this polling to a member of the sales team. It seems logical to assign it to them, but it is a big mistake. Part of the problem may *be* the sales team. You want someone who is independent, a very good listener, and inquisitive enough to get to the bottom of what is happening. Oftentimes, a retired marketing person is a good person to do this, if hired on a part-time basis.

This process should be begun as soon as possible and concluded before you set your main plan in motion. The feedback that you will get will allow you to move forward, and work on the things that matter.

Each company will face unique circumstances, but the operational issues discussed in section two are ones that I have found to be consistent issues in most failing businesses. Here are the topics that we are going to cover in the second section of this book:

- Vision
- Holding people accountable for results
- Measurements of performance
- Goals and objectives
- Bonuses
- Gross margin analysis
- Business unit segmentation
- Quality
- New business development

Now, I am not saying that if you do these things and these things only that you can effectively turn your business around. These issues were the ones that were common to all four businesses with which I was involved.

In each business, however, we did many other things specific to our circumstances. You will have to as well. Circumstances may dictate specific tactics that you will have to utilize. These may include such things as looking to competitors for good ideas, implementing best practices, revising procedures, etc.

Effectively addressing these issues, however, helped turn around all four of the businesses I faced. There are some common themes here. Effectively addressing these issues helped our results tremendously. Hopefully, some of these can help you, too.

Summary

You must now turn your attention to thinking about the operational issues that you must face and change to turn around your company. First, it will be imperative to figure out exactly what needs to be corrected, and this means talking to current and lost customers in addition to people within the organization. If you do not get the view of those outside the group, you are not likely to get a complete, accurate picture of what needs to be done. Every failing company will have unique circumstances; there is no formula for you to follow. That is why it is your responsibility to investigate all angles of the company's circumstance to determine relevant tactics for improvement.

Chapter Twelve
Workbook

- How have you attempted to gain feedback on the company's operations from employees?

_____

_____

_____

_____

- How have you gained feedback from customers, both current and lost?

_____

_____

_____

_____

- What were the major concerns that you uncovered through these two sources?

_____

_____

_____

_____

_____

_____

CHAPTER THIRTEEN

VISION

One of the first things you must do is to create a vision for your business. Another one of my rules is: **Unless you know where you want to take your business, you will never get there**. A vision statement plainly expresses the direction, goals, and principles of the organization. The vision can serve as a guide for your business; all employees are rallied behind a common goal, and each person knows exactly what to strive toward. In this way, it gives the group focus and can guide all decisions.

The first question you must ask is, "What business am I in?" That sounds simplistic, but it is the core to the vision that you have. It is the direction the company will take and, as a result, the fate the company will have.

When asked what their business is, most people will respond by identifying what it does: "a manufacturer of widgets," "a wholesaler of gizmos," or "a retailer of what-chamacallits." These statements are superficial because they do not describe how or why your business functions. In order to effectively define what business you are in, you must look at these issues:

- Who are your customers and what are their needs?
- What products do you offer (tangible and intangible)?
- What method of product delivery or distribution do you use?
- What pricing structure do you use?
- What emphasis on quality do you have?
- What is extra or unique about your business?
- Why are you better than your competition?
- What things does your competition do better?

Once you have this image set, then and only then are you ready to create a vision for the company. Sure, it is grandiose and impressive to speak of being the industry leader in producing the highest quality widgets, but if you have a three-person shop with older equipment, maybe your vision should be directed in another area, such as a custom widget maker that works hands-on to produce all manner of special widgets.

A vision is a mental picture of the desired future state of what you want your business to look like. For example, you can focus on competing on quality and service. You can try and cut costs and be the low-price supplier. Ideally, you would like to be able to do both. If you were both the low-cost and the high-quality supplier and the best service supplier, you wouldn't be reading this book; you would have more business than you could handle.

You must make a conscious decision as to what strategy will best address the needs of your business in your current circumstances. It is mind-boggling how many businesses don't have a clue about where they want to go. They try to attack everything and, as a result, accomplish nothing.

It is also important that your vision encompass the defining principles of your company. How are customers and employees to be treated? What are your main priorities? What is most important to the organization? When a vision outlines these objectives, it can greatly aid decision making and problem solving. Everyone in the organization will be aware of the big-picture concerns.

Revitalizing a business isn't just about plugging the leaks; it is also about choosing the right direction in which to take the business. When the business is badly leaking and about to sink, it is difficult to make radical course direction changes. Yet this may be precisely what is needed.

Before the business goes on doing what has obviously gotten it in trouble, you must assess: (1) was the problem the course, or (2) was the problem the way the business took that course. These are very tough issues to divide, especially without the luxury of time and hindsight. You are thrust into a position where the boat is rapidly taking in water and the immediate priority may be to man the bilge pumps. Do not allow yourself to get caught in somebody else's bad business vision. Assess that up front.

Don't make the mistake of forming the vision for the business in a vacuum. If you do, while it will be your vision, there will not be a wide base of support for it, and it will probably fail. You must at least engage your key managers in the creation of the vision statement for the business. You must make it "our vision" for the business.

Andrew Harvey, in his book *The Call to Lead*, explained how a strong vision gives confidence to the entire organization. He wrote, "The vision serves to unify the organization with a shared purpose. This communal goal gives a sense of commitment and focus to every member of an organization and motivates them to fulfill the aspirations of the vision." Without direction, you cannot hope to achieve long-term success and stability.

The mistake made with most vision statements is that they are too long. It should be able to fit nicely on the back of your business card. If it cannot, it is probably too long. Your troops have got to be able to remember it and recite it clearly. A simple example like "Quality is job #1" worked very nicely for Ford Motor Co.

Make sure that your vision is clearly communicated and that it addresses a vital business issue where you can create a sense of urgency around it. If there isn't a sense of urgency to achieve your vision, it won't get achieved. It can't just be your sense of urgency; it has to be the whole team's sense of urgency. It has got to ignite the troops. The vision has to create a cause that the organization can willingly support.

Summary

You must make sure that everyone in the company knows and understands the vision. It will not do any good framed on the wall; it must be incorporated into daily life within the organization. It is management's responsibility to continually reiterate the vision statement to employees. It must be communicated clearly and frequently. Once everyone understands it, the vision can be used to create practices, goals, and objectives. It will permeate all aspects of the company.

Knowing where you want to go is critical. It provides direction to the entire organization. The fact of the matter is that this is one of the most important jobs that you can do.

Chapter Thirteen
Workbook

- Most people confuse a vision statement with a mission statement. How does a vision statement differ from a mission statement?

_____

_____

_____

_____

_____

- Why is it important to include your key people in the development of your vision statement?

_____

_____

_____

_____

_____

- Write out your vision statement.

_____

_____

_____

_____

_____

- How do you plan on communicating the vision so that everyone understands and follows it?

_____

_____

_____

_____

_____

- How has the vision statement been incorporated into the daily life of your organization?

_____

_____

_____

_____

_____

CHAPTER FOURTEEN

HOLDING PEOPLE ACCOUNTABLE FOR RESULTS

I am amazed by how widespread the lack of personal responsibility is in many businesses. Without exception, key people in organizations that are failing are not held accountable for results. Now, let me make it very clear that I am not saying that they aren't given performance appraisals. What I am saying is that the performance appraisals and the bonuses that result from them are not usually tied directly to the results of the business. Sounds strange, doesn't it? Yeah, I thought so, too, until I encountered it over and over again.

A business that I was recently asked to turn around lost 50% of its sales overnight as the two offshore sister plants came on stream and began to manufacture their own products. The remaining business was failing and not making money. The sales manager I inherited hadn't opened a new account in more than a year. Furthermore, he didn't have a single "hot prospect" pending. Yet, he was given an acceptable performance review and a decent bonus. Go figure.

This wasn't a lone exception by a long shot. The plant manager didn't know what was happening on the plant floor, didn't get or ask for production reports, and didn't track cost per unit. He was an autocratic manager who utilized fear and intimidation. Yet, while his review alluded to these issues, he was given an acceptable performance evaluation and a decent bonus.

The plant controller was just plain incapable. He didn't have formal financial training and wasn't contributing financial advice to the business. He couldn't analyze manufacturing costs effectively. Yet, we were paying him as much as the plant manager and gave him a huge bonus.

The plant supervisors, just as in most plants I have had to turn around as well as those that are doing reasonably well, were glorified babysitters. They were not responsible for production results, quality, or safety. They didn't have to discipline their employees, nor were they required to hold their people accountable for results. Needless to say, they didn't have to fire anyone either.

Is it any wonder that we had a sea of apathy? The sad truth is that putting training aside, the plant supervisors in the businesses that I have had to come in and run were not being judged as to how they contributed to results. The people under them were being given performance reviews and wage increases without any objective reference to their production. None of their employees had production goals, either collectively as a team or individually.

In a plant I ran in the South, the plant manager and I had the machinists, the people who set up and changed our machines from product to product, take the Bennetts Mechanical Aptitude Test. We then correlated the results with the performance appraisals.

Guess what we found! There was a direct, inverse relationship to how they scored on the aptitude test and their performance appraisals. The machinists who scored the lowest on the aptitude tests were the ones considered to be the highest skilled, highest performing adjusters.

How could this be? What was happening was that the performance appraisals weren't based on hard production and change time data. The machinist who didn't give the supervisors grief and the ones who worked overtime when needed were being given the best performance appraisals.

The most skilled ones, the ones who scored the highest on the aptitude test, had the lower performance appraisals because they knew enough to give supervisors grief when they wouldn't do preventative maintenance or batch jobs effectively to minimize change times, etc.

This mind-boggling experience led me to check to see if plant managers and supervisors had production goals or not. Amazingly, in most plants I have been asked to run, they did not, nor did any of the hourly plant employees. This is a real problem. If your plant management, including supervisors, does not have specific production, quality, and safety goals and are not being held accountable to meet them, you can pretty well conclude that you have a problem. It sounds so basic, but given the prevalence of this condition, it isn't unusual.

Accountability, however, is a much more global issue than just the manufacturing plant floor. It applies to sales, plant controllers, customer service, technical staff, human resources, and on and on.

One of the most common conditions of failing organizations is that they cannot get anything done. It is attributable to resources—that is to say, money or people. It is usually attributable to a combination of problems: lack of accountability, not establishing formal written goals, not tracking results for goals, and not knowing how to construct action plans to achieve those goals.

Managers and supervisors who do not want to confront difficult and uncomfortable issues like sub-par performance usually cause the lack of accountability. It is amazing how many managers will not be honest in appraising their employees and do not give them constructive criticism. They avoid this like the plague. It is also amazing how prevalent this practice is!

Most private business owners can be described as benevolent dictators. They want absolute power, but they also want to be popular. Their management style can be described as follows:

- They spend a lot of money on picnics, Christmas parties, etc.

- Their organizations are usually overstaffed.

- Their organizations aren't held accountable for results.

- Their key managers do not have specifically defined objectives each year.

- They do not allow their managers to participate in most decision making.

- They tend to pinch pennies in some areas and blow big bucks in others without justifying the benefits.

Most owners of companies have never had formal managerial or leadership training. While some are good at it, most are not. Just because they invested the capital to own businesses does not mean that they can run them effectively. Since they have not been properly trained in managing and leading, they don't know that they aren't good managers or leaders. Since they are the owners, they don't normally solicit feedback and input, so they will never know.

The lack of accountability has been prominent in all four businesses that I have transformed. Managers and supervisors have been allowed to ignore performance issues, which has disastrous effects. This is probably the single biggest issue in businesses that are failing.

Another of my rules is: **To turn a business around, you must achieve accountability for performance from the very top of the organization all the way down to the very bottom.** Accountability for performance starts, of course, at the managerial level. You must improve the level of your manager's performance or your business will fail. You must then make sure that managers are holding their own people accountable for performance and right on down the line.

So how does one establish accountability? It begins by having a business plan that lays out objectives for the organization as a whole and for each department or unit of the organization. We are not talking about the kind of business plans that a business might parade in front of lenders and venture capitalists; those tend to be dog and pony shows with little relevance to the day to day. The kind of business plan we want is one that sets specific overall objectives. Each department or unit within the business should have a list of objectives. Each goal must have a "metric," or a way of measuring its accomplishments. To just say that you want to "improve customer satisfaction" is meaningless because it is too broad and difficult to measure. A better goal would be "improve customer satisfaction with product quality from 83% to 90% as measured by past sales surveys."

The manager or officer responsible for the goal or objective must have something to say about the for-mulation of the goal and also must be accountable for the goal's realization. There have to be consequences, like no bonus or reduction of perks, that are related to the failure to achieve the goal. If performance is not measured by some objective measurement then it is left to opinion and conjecture.

Similarly, the goal/objective/measurement process has to extend to virtually everyone on the payroll. Sometimes it is difficult to pin down performance by person, but a good manager has the responsibility to do so. Sometimes, performance has to be measured based on small teams. If effectively done, the accountability issue is very motivating for employees. They see the results of their efforts affecting their compensation. They have a reason to put out 100% effort.

On the other hand, standards that are ill conceived, arbitrarily imposed, and ineffectively managed can back-fire badly. Employees will soon figure out how to "game" a situation while ignoring the bigger picture. In the worst case, the imposition of goal measurement can result in rebellion. As in most things, a delicate balance exists in imposing standards, setting goals and objectives cooperatively, and then measuring and interpreting the results.

Summary

Accountability is a company-wide concern. It must permeate every level of your organization. Most failing businesses suffer from not being able to get things done, and this is a problem of accountability. To combat this issue, you must create specific, measurable goals and track results objectively. Unless employees see the correlation between their efforts and their compensation, they may have little motivating them to work to their potential.

Chapter Fourteen
Workbook

- How can you determine whether or not you have accountability for performance?

_____

_____

_____

_____

- Do your supervisors, team leaders, and operators have specific, quantitative production, quality, and safety goals? What are they? If they do not have any, why not?

_____

_____

_____

_____

_____

- How do you measure the performances of your employees?

_____

_____

_____

_____

- Do you have specific, objective, measurable goals to measure your managers, supervisors, team leaders, and sales representatives? What are they? If not, why not?

  _____

  _____

  _____

  _____

  _____

- Do you match the profile of a benevolent dictator? If so, do you want to change your leadership style? If so, what changes do you intend to make?

  _____

  _____

  _____

  _____

  _____

CHAPTER FIFTEEN

THE BAD APPLE

Now that we have talked about holding people accountable, the next personnel issue you must deal with is the "bad apple." In most organizations, you have one such person. In turnaround situations, you usually have many because one of the key reasons the business is in trouble is usually that managers and supervisors haven't addressed the tough, unpleasant people issues. This is why it is on your plate rather than having been resolved already. So, resolve it you must.

The bad apple is normally a deviant leader. He or she is the one on the plant floor who has the most influence over people. The source of this influence can be technical knowledge, personal connections, or seniority. Most likely, however, it will be their personalities. They are usually very vocal in break rooms and on the floor. They usually don't speak up at meetings, however, because they are interested in their agenda, not yours. This is what makes them deviant leaders.

Yes, you must try to work with them and gain their support. I wish I could tell you I've had more success with this problem than I have had. Changing deviant leaders into positive leaders can be done, but it takes a tremendous amount of time and energy. Even at that, there isn't any guarantee that you will be successful.

Why then even deal with the bad apple? They can, and in most cases will, become a significant impediment to your efforts to achieve employee involvement and teamwork. They want to maintain the status quo. Why? The answer is that they want to maintain their level of influence. You see, maintaining their influence is more important to them than your business being successful. They are also generally cunning and devious. They will not make their efforts and feelings known to you. They generally conduct their efforts to torpedo your initiatives in secret. Since they are trying to make you fail, their efforts are beneath the surface. Yet they have so much influence that they can have a serious impact upon your morale.

The first thing you must do is find out who these bad apples are. How do you do that? You do it by forming good relationships with enough floor people that at least one, if not many, will share that information with you. Without a good relationship with good employees who see the need for change and who are concerned about the welfare of the business, it will be very difficult to identify those employees who are trying to maintain the status quo or even worse, who are trying make your efforts fail.

Once you identify these bad apples, you must confront them. While it would be nice to be able to tell you that you can confront them on their productivity or attendance issues, the truth is that in most cases you are going to have to confront them on their behavior and attitude. This is where it gets very difficult. Most employees will not willingly get involved in interpersonal issues with co-workers much less the deviant leaders. So while you can use the information from co-workers to identify the deviant leader, seldom can you use this testimony to confront them.

The important point here is that in some cases it will be almost impossible to identify the bad apples and even harder to pin them down and hold them accountable. Part of the problem will stem from the perceived divide between management and worker. The workers, as a group, will react in the same way as children on the school ground when a teacher tries to find out who threw the baseball at the school window. No one will know anything. They don't want to be "stool pigeons" of management. I would suggest that there is no way to overcome this reluctance short of befriending your workers on a one-on-one basis. It will be necessary to gain their confidence and then find out what is really happening.

Some management consultants claim that they can identify the "factory bullies" by psychological profile. That is an expensive and iffy proposition.

How do you deal with suspected bad apples? The most direct approach is to confront them on it. There are a couple of ways in which you can confront them on their behavior. With one bad apple, we found that he wouldn't help his teammates change their printing press. We confronted him on this specific work behavior, which was having a huge negative impact on the morale and productivity of the plant. By holding him accountable for his behavior associated with his job duties, we were able to effectively address his attempt to torpedo teamwork. We were able to make his behavior a performance issue.

Obviously, to avoid costly litigation you must document, document, document. Otherwise, forget it.

Another way to address behavior, while more difficult and not always successful, is through the "group of coworkers" approach. Instead of being able to quote a specific person's observation of the undesirable behavior, you indicate to the deviant leader that *many* employees have told you about this behavior.

First of all, you cannot invent these accusations. They must be real. I confirmed the attempt of one bad apple to have all three shifts of an entire department call off from work one day. I heard this from at least three sources on the plant floor. I confirmed with the business unit manager that he had heard the same thing from at least three different co-workers.

The business unit manager and I sat down to confront the deviant leader. We both indicated that we had individually heard from several employees about his efforts to initiate a "call-off" and that we weren't about to put up with that type of behavior. He didn't deny it but rather hid behind his contention that he wasn't alone and that several employees were behind it.

We didn't let him off the hook while he tried to divert our attention away from him. We didn't yell at him. We spoke to him softly and politely and looked him dead in the eye and said, "This is totally unacceptable." You could see him turn white with anxiety.

This employee was a very muscular, stocky man who often wore cut-off shirts. His physical presence intimidated people. For the first time in more than twenty years, someone had the courage to confront him and tell him to his face that enough was enough. He quickly folded his tent and stopped causing problems.

Were we on friendly terms after that? No, I had to pull "good afternoon" out of him and really couldn't get much more than that. However, what we got was much more important than niceties. We received accountability from him and an end to his undermining tactics.

Summary

In the end, it may be that you only have suspicions about who your bad apples are. It may be impossible to identify them, much less confront them with issues that may have little or no supporting documentation.

One approach that sometimes works is to isolate them. If you can have them work alone, that is ideal. If not, change their assigned department or shift. Moving them to a new and unfamiliar situation puts them in a position where they can be the "new person."

Another approach is to pit them against one another. Assign them all to the same team, put some pressure on, and see who pops first. When you put all the bad apples together amazingly you sometimes get applesauce.

Chapter Fifteen
Workbook

- Why is it necessary to address the behaviors of the bad apple?

_____

_____

_____

- Why is it important to form good relationships with employees? How do you initiate these relationships?

_____

_____

_____

_____

_____

- What are some ways in which you can effectively address the behaviors of the bad apple?

_____

_____

_____

_____

_____

_____

CHAPTER SIXTEEN

SETTING PRIORITIES

One of the most critical personal performance objectives an organization needs to achieve is managing priorities. It has absolutely amazed me how many bright managers, some with MBAs, do not know how to manage their priorities. So many managers in organizations that are failing spend most of their time fire fighting.

As Stephen Covey said in his book, *The Seven Habits of Highly Effective People,* so many managers spend their time on problems and opportunities that are urgent but relatively unimportant. People showing up on their doorstep cause the majority of these diversions. Saying no to somebody face to face seems to be much more difficult for most people. As a result, so many managers and supervisors spend time fire fighting and not working on the key projects that will move the business forward.

What are the common causes for this seemingly senseless behavior? Basically, people's work habits are *extremely hard to change.* Just like going on a diet or giving up smoking, changing a work habit is equally as tough.

Managing your priorities and working on the *most important* items isn't difficult, unless you haven't developed this habit. You see, writing to-do lists and prioritizing them takes effort and self-discipline. Even though it makes managers more effective and their work more manageable, it amazes me how many bright, intelligent managers have never developed the self-discipline to manage their own priorities and determine where and how they spend their time.

How can this be? The best explanation I can give is that for whatever reason they have never learned good technique. For some reason, they have never been taught how to do this or they refuse to put in the extra time and effort to do so. Most of the time spent developing to-do lists and prioritizing them is spent at home. It is absolutely amazing how many managers in businesses that are failing are unwilling to put in this "extra" time.

Whether the lack of prioritization is a result of a lack of technique or a lack of willingness, the result is still the same. You end up with ineffective managers. Obviously you cannot live with this situation. One of the most obvious signs of poor self-management is that projects are late or that they simply fall through the cracks and are not being worked on at all. Managers with poor self-management tend to either be late for meetings or miss them all together.

While you can work with them through formal training, as they say, teaching an old dog new tricks is difficult. One way to get them into the habit of prioritizing is to review their to-do lists with them frequently. It can be every two weeks or more frequently if necessary. You can then ensure that they are working on the correct objectives.

In your one-on-one reviews, make sure that you have agreement on timelines and expected outcomes. Always, always ask your people for timelines for the projects on which they are working. Also, have written expectations of what the results will look like.

The best starting point that I have found is to share your own personal goals and objectives for the coming year with your managers. Have interactive discussions with them as a group so that they understand why these goals are important. Then, their own goals and objectives should support and complement your goals and objectives so that they are integrated. You can achieve this by developing the goals and objectives as a group or by giving them the goals you have developed on your own. You will have to be the judge as to which alternative is more effective in your situation.

Another strange characteristic in some managers of failing businesses is the inability to proactively identify issues and opportunities. While this sounds strange, and it is, it isn't all that uncommon. These managers wait for problems to come to them rather than take the time and effort to identify issues and opportunities on which they could work. As a result, they are totally reactive—that is, they simply deal with the problems and issues that find a way to their doorstep. It is as if they adopt a bunker mentality and are afraid to come out lest another bombshell goes off near them.

Since these managers do not have the mental discipline to identify what should be done, they cannot effectively prioritize what should be addressed first. They simply use a FIFO system (first in, first out). Sound strange? Yeah, that is what I thought, too. Unfortunately, it isn't all that uncommon.

How do you deal with this kind of manager? It depends upon how dire your situation is and what things you need this manager to accomplish for you. One option is to stay on top of this type of manager and review the person's to-do lists as well as his or her priorities on a weekly basis. Another alternative is to fire this person early on and cut your losses. Another alternative is to put this person through extensive training and development. The last alternative is to simply live with it. You will have to decide which one makes the most sense for you.

While you should have quarterly reviews of your team's formal goals and objectives, having biweekly reviews of their priorities is also extremely beneficial. Most organizations are ineffective because key managers get diverted into issues and problems that, while urgent, in the scheme of things aren't very important. Combine this with a lack of accountability for their results and what you have is an under-performing organization. When you have an under-performing organization for any length of time, you aren't very far away from a crisis.

One way to keep a handle on the status of to do's is to have managers post them on a company-wide database. This allows a coordination of plans, objectives, and to do's. Using project planning and control software for this purpose also keeps the organization firmly focused on the overall objective.

Summary

When you are in a crisis, you have to make multiple "systemic fixes." You have to get the organization going and get it going forward quickly. When things haven't been getting done for so long, you cannot expect to have things happen just because you and your management team have discussed it and the key players have agreed to do it.

You must monitor your team's focus and their progress to ensure that *things are getting done*. You cannot afford to find out four months later that the project hasn't even gotten started. While this dilemma seems implausible, trust me when I say that it is the rule rather than the exception. Get after prioritization early on and keep after it. It is how your organization will keep your business from extinction.

Chapter Sixteen
Workbook

- Are your key managers, supervisors, and team leaders setting written objectives, keeping written to-do lists, and prioritizing them? If not, why not? If so, are you reviewing them regularly? How often do you review them? How do you evaluate these lists?

_____

_____

_____

_____

_____

_____

_____

- Are your key managers habitually late with their projects? Why do you think this problem is occurring? How have you been dealing with this? If you haven't dealt with it, why not?

_____

_____

_____

_____

_____

CHAPTER SEVENTEEN

"METRICS"

The four businesses that I have had to turn around all suffered from a lack of good measurements. Most of them had good accounting and financial reporting. We knew the score and knew we were losing. We knew if we needed more sales or if our material costs were above or below budget. We knew if our labor costs or overtime costs were above or below budget. Yet, all four businesses had lousy measurements! How can this be, you ask?

First of all, they weren't measuring the right stuff. More importantly, they did not have effective action plans to improve the results of the things that they weren't measuring. The moral of the story here is that **you don't know what you don't know!** If you are not measuring the right stuff, you can bet that it isn't improving!

Spend time figuring out what needs to be measured. Some of the common issues that need to be measured and are not necessarily always focused on are:

- Manufacturing cost per unit of output
- Waste (per job for custom businesses, per stock number for standard products)
- Quality
- Safety
- Sales cost per sale
- Sales dollars versus budget
- Headcount/Productivity measurements
- Margin percents by business segment, customer, product line, or stock number
- Percentage ROS or ROI by segment, product line, or SKU

Some of the more subtle but significant measurements that need to be focused on are:

- On-time deliveries

  I took over a custom products business doing quite well, or so they thought. They never measured on-time deliveries. They were shocked to find out that one-third of their shipments were habitually late.

- New business development

  Even though most failing businesses need more sales, not one I took over formally tracked new business or had targets for number of new customers, dollar amount targets for new business, number of appointments per week, etc.

- Service

  This is how customers rated our service, things like flexibility, responsiveness, and reliability versus our competitors.

- Sales effectiveness

  This is how professional and helpful our sales reps were versus our competition.

The key here is to step back and ask what things must really be done well in order to be successful. This step goes back to our discussion of vision: What business is the company in? From that analysis should come a list of things that the company needs to do to reach its objectives. Some are not obvious. This is where brainstorming with your leadership team can really help. Once you decide what areas are most important, measure the heck out of them and pay attention to the feedback you get!

In most businesses, measurements come down to only a few things. Many companies waste too many resources to measure things that are irrelevant. They generate reams of reports that are never really used. A good reporting system creates only those reports that are important. It also contains measurements that, like the "idiot lights" on a car dashboard, only go off if something is wrong.

The reports should be circulated only to those who need them—in other words, those people who can take action to change things. One very successful company limited each manager's reports to no more than five. The CEO got only five sheets of paper every two weeks. That was the extent of reporting. It was a finely tuned reporting machine that relied upon systems that were well thought out and executed. Needless to say, the company is very efficient and profitable.

Should you hire a management consultant to help you evaluate the status of your system? Hiring an outsider has its pluses and minuses, but the decision comes down to the resources available and the urgency of the situation. Oftentimes, a good CPA can be retained to review the status of the reporting system. While absolute reliance cannot be placed on one consultant, they can be a valuable source for fresh, independent input.

Summary

Before you can improve the things that are causing the business to fail, you must know what those things are. It will take time and probably group effort to determine what must be measured. Think beyond the obvious, like labor costs and material costs, which are probably already being measured. Once you find areas that need corrections, define specific goals for improvement and create specific action plans that will help accomplish these goals. This is probably another area where brainstorming and team input will be beneficial. Without targeting and attacking the specific areas that need improvement, a successful turnaround is not likely to occur.

Chapter Seventeen
Workbook

• What are the key results in your business that you are tracking? How are you tracking them?

_____

_____

_____

_____

_____

• Have you identified the key result areas of your business that need improvement? What are they and what measurements are you going to use?

Key Result Area Measurement

1. _____

_____

2. _____

_____

3. _____

_____

4. _____

_____

5. _____

_____

CHAPTER EIGHTEEN

PERFORMANCE REVIEWS AND BONUSES

This chapter is about what kinds of things most failing businesses neglect to do with performance appraisals. First of all, most failing business do not have objective measurements of performance. They allude to "doing a good job," whatever that means. Without clear, quantitative measurements of performance, most failing organizations do not rate performance in their performance reviews. What they rate are perceptions of performance, which are usually inaccurate and/or ineffective.

If your bonuses are based upon objective, quantifiable goals, your performance reviews should be based upon the same criteria. Without specific, objective, quantifiable operating criteria, assessing performance is usually based upon relationships and personal chemistry. These perceptions usually distort reality rather than reflect it.

Performance reviews should be done in a standard, systemized manner. All employees must have clearly defined job requirements, and reviews should reflect performance based upon these criteria. In this way, bonuses and promotions are systemized and reflect actual performance, not seniority or personal connections.

For this system to work, management must define and clearly communicate specific measurements of performance and job requirements. This should be done anyway to maximize productivity. Too often, workers are told things like "we need to increase sales." To most workers, this means very little. However, if you tell them to increase sales by 10% within a specific time period, they have a firm, objective goal to work toward. Then, reviewing performance is simplified to a standard measurement of how well this goal was accomplished. This practice will most likely give employees more faith in the review process because it will be judged as fair and objective.

Having quantifiable, standardized performance reviews will also motivate workers and stave off apathy. Reviews will be directly related to actual performance and objective perceptions of performance. This creates a fair environment for reviews, raises, and promotions and helps keep morale high within the organization.

To give effective performance appraisals, make sure you are rating the right stuff. I talk more about goals and objectives in the next chapter.

The other critical performance review practice most businesses, whether failing or not, do wrong is for the manager to write the review and submit it along with salary action to his or her boss before it is ever reviewed with the employee. **Always, always review the appraisal with the employee first before submitting it to your boss.**

Why do I say this? Reviewing the appraisal with the employee first provides you with the opportunity to get good feedback. This means that the employee can change your perception on some things with facts and information that you didn't have when you wrote the appraisal. To be fair, you must be willing to modify the appraisal with new and better information.

Once you submit it to your boss, you are locked in to your position. Not only can you not change it, but also you risk creating an adversarial review with your employee when he or she feels that you are being unfair. Remember, an appraisal is a two-way street. You will be giving the employee some feedback that is new information to him or her, and the employee will be giving you feedback and new information as well. If your performance appraisals are not working this way, I would recommend that you consider changing the format in order to accomplish this. Why put yourself and the employee in the above position? **Simply don't do it!**

Summary

Make sure you are reviewing the right stuff in regards to a person's performance by comparing his or her results to quantifiable goals. Focus on results, not on activity. Make sure that you are rewarding people on outcomes rather than on stuff that isn't improving your results. Also make sure that you review the appraisal with the employee before you submit it to your boss. Be willing to modify the review and the salary action based upon the feedback you get from the employee.

Chapter Eighteen
Workbook

- Why is it important to review your employees' performance appraisal with them before submitting the performance appraisal and salary increase to your boss for approval?

_____

_____

_____

_____

- How can you ensure that you are reviewing employees' performances based on the "right stuff"? (Try reviewing their quantifiable results versus their goals.)

_____

_____

_____

_____

- How do you define and communicate job requirements? Are these requirements specific and geared toward improving the company?

_____

_____

_____

CHAPTER NINETEEN

BONUSES,GOALS,AND OBJECTIVES

The principles surrounding bonuses, goals, and objectives are pretty straightforward, yet it is amazing how many businesses get it wrong. You must not only tie bonuses directly to the results that you want, but you must also define how they must accomplish these results. Unlike what some employees seem to believe, a bonus should be a reward for extraordinary work results, not an entitlement.

One business I took over that was going down the tube at warp speed paid their top management 50% of their bonuses on the profit performance of the total business. While this is pretty standard stuff, they didn't define how it could be generated. The business was making products for their sister plants overseas. The division controller, who also worked directly for this business and whose bonus was directly impacted by their profit results, arranged to transfer 50% of their sales to the two sister plants at high margins.

The business did not find new external customers, did not develop new business, charged the customers of their sister plants higher prices than were budgeted, and yet the management got paid obscene bonuses. I mean really obscene, since their budget did not forecast their shipping products overseas at high margins. Worse yet, when the overseas shipments stopped the month after I got there, 50% of their business went out the door without so much as a prospect in the pipeline. The management left the business in a situation where it would start losing money immediately. Yet, they received obscene bonuses for "beating their income budget."

The lesson here is that you must always define how the goal must be achieved—that is, by their own efforts and not by a windfall. This gets back to the original problem of setting objective measurements. It is too simplistic to base the performance bonus on sales, productivity, or one figure alone. The setting of goals involves many factors, all of which must come together to produce the desired success of the company. In the end, the performance appraisal may hinge on a number of factors. The evaluator may have to make an estimate as to the percentage to which goals were accomplished. How goals and objectives are achieved is as important as achieving them.

The other big mistake many businesses make is to offer incentives to their managers on activity rather than on results, for example, opening X number of new accounts. Well, if it turns out that they are all small accounts worth a thousand dollars annually, what have you accomplished? Tie the reward specifically to the results needed by your business, provided that they are fair expectations.

Fair means that the manager and the employee mutually set the goals. I had a boss set my goals for me and submit them without ever reviewing them with me. I diplomatically pointed out that many of them were the wrong goals and that others were unrealistic. Don't do this to your people! Gaining their commitment for achieving aggressive goals is one of the most important things a good manager can achieve. Merely putting down on paper what you would like to happen is not only meaningless, but it also causes your people's motivation to drop.

The other requirement for good goals and objectives is that they must be quantifiable and measurable. If you cannot measure the desired results with hard data, they are more than likely not good goals. Eliminate as much subjectivity from them as you can.

Another common mistake some companies make is that their goals are locked in concrete and cannot change based on the needs of the business. Key managers spend time trying to accomplish obsolete objectives. Let your people change their objectives provided that you review and approve the new goals. Always make sure that they are working on the right stuff and being given incentives and rewards for meeting or exceeding the right goals. The key here is that when they revise their goals, don't let them set a target that is too low. Since half the year is probably gone, the goal cannot be something, for example, that they already accomplished. It must be for a future event.

Revising a sales target, for example, for some big customers that you have obtained is fine as long as the new total year target incorporates these new accounts into the new target. The revised goal, therefore, is just as challenging as the old one. Don't revise the sales goal, however, just because you got some huge new accounts. If they earned them, reward them for it. If they were handed to them, then revise their goals.

Summary

Compensation and performance issues can be two of the most contentious issues that face management. In a struggling enterprise, the problems are only magnified.

People need to have the right goals and objectives. These goals should be definite, objective, and measurable. The results of an employee's performance review should be the consensus conclusion of the employee and the manager.

Bonuses and raises should come as the result of meeting the predefined objectives. A clear and logical relationship between the employee's performance and compensation is essential to the esprit de corps of any organization and can go a long way toward moving the company to profitability.

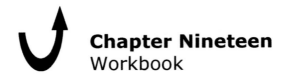

Chapter Nineteen
Workbook

- How do you tie bonuses to results versus activity?

_____

_____

_____

_____

- Do you define how your people must accomplish their results? What types of guidelines do you set?

_____

_____

_____

_____

_____

- Are your goals and objectives set mutually with your people or do you give them their goals? Which way is more effective?

_____

_____

_____

_____

_____

- Are your goals and the results accomplished measurable and quantifiable?

  _____

  _____

  _____

  _____

  _____

- Do you review your goals at midyear and make changes? If so, how do you decide how to change them?

  _____

  _____

  _____

  _____

  _____

- How do you know whether or not your people's goals are focused on the "right stuff"? (Hint: If your people accomplish their goals, will your business achieve its key objectives?)

  _____

  _____

  _____

  _____

  _____

CHAPTER TWENTY

ANALYSIS OF PRODUCT MARGINS AND PRICING

Custom vs. Standard Products in a Manufacturing Environment

Manufacturers face unique problems costing and selling their products. In the simplest situation, there is the issue of making standard products every day or pursuing custom or job shop products. There is some confusion surrounding the pricing of these two distinct products.

One of the most important things to understand is how custom products impact your cost and your profitability. The key characteristic that distinguishes a custom product from a standard product is *set-up time*. The fatal flaw most businesses that make custom or special products make is in the pricing. Most sophisticated businesses correctly cost each job by charging the addi- tional set-up time to the cost of the special item. For example, if the set-up time is six hours and the machine hour rate is $150 an hour, $900 of set-up time is added to the cost.

The fatal flaw is that most businesses then mark up the special or job shop by about the same margin percent. The logic being that if you mark up your set-up costs, you're not only recovering your additional costs but making a profit on it, too. Well, you are, but while you are making the same amount of margin percent, you will not make the same amount of margin dollars.

This is difficult to understand without looking at two side-by-side analyses (shown below). The fallacy that many businesses make is that they do their analyses based on percents and profit margins when what is important is the total dollar profit. Remember, **you do not take margin percents to the bank.**

The flaw in the logic here is that while you are marking up your set-up time while you are not running, you are losing the margin mark up on your materials. Let's look at an example:

	Scenario #1 (Standard)	Scenario #2 (Special)
Materials	$5.00/M	$5.00/M
Labor	$2.00/M	$2.00/M
Overhead	$2.00/M	$2.00/M
Set-up Costs	0	$0.90/M
Total Costs	$9.00/M	$9.90/M
Margin @ 30%	$3.86/M	$4.24/M
Selling Price	$12.86/M	$14.14/M
Quantity	1.0 Million	1.0 Million
Run Time	27.8 Hrs	27.8 Hrs
Set-up Time	0	9.0 Hrs
Total Time	27.8 Hrs	36.8 Hrs
Sales Dollars	$12,860	$14,140
Margin Dollars	$3,860	$4,240
Margin Percent	30%	30%
Margin per Machine Hour	$139	$115

The point here is that while you are setting up the special in scenario #2 you could be running standard products, as seen in scenario #1. Running the machine for 36.8 hours in scenario #1 will generate $5,115 margin dollars. You will make more money running standard products for the same amount of *total elapsed time*, even though you are making the same margin percents. This difference is subtle but significant. Most controllers cannot make this distinction. All too often, pricing decisions are made by margin percents. My rule is: **Not all margin percents are created equal.** To put it another way, there is an "opportunity cost" in doing special jobs instead of keeping the shop producing the same standard products hour after hour.

You must know the difference in profit rates between specials and stock products. You have to look at total throughput and margin *dollar* generation. You then must price your specials to be able to generate the same absolute dollar profit as your stock. You must also take into consideration that your scrap rates will be higher on specials and that your average run speeds will be lower as you ramp the machine up.

You must price each special by job and price these specials to be at least as profitable in absolute margin per machine hour as the standard products. We will also talk about small custom jobs and large jobs and how they impact your costs and profits a little later. If you are pricing your jobs off of total plant costs and fixed overhead rates, you really have a serious problem, one with which your plant controller should be able to help you.

Having run multiple plants making custom products, I now know that this is a key procedure that you must learn and apply. As an example, my plant was running about 50% specials and 50% stock. Our sister plant three hours away was running 95% stock and 5% specials. This plant was making more money than we were. Our floor people could set up machines much more efficiently, could set up a much wider range of features, and produce better quality work. However, because specials had specific due dates, specific specifications, and specific print requirements, customer complaints on specials outweighed stock items about ten to one. Our plant had a much higher technical skill level, a much higher level of production skill, and higher product quality.

It was because our sister plant had more throughput, more equipment, almost no set-up time, and few customer complaints that they were deemed to be better managed and had better customer service. The truth is that they could never do what we were doing. Upper management couldn't distinguish the difference. I was faced with trying to overcome years of charging our biggest customers prices on custom products that were too low to allow us to make a similar profit. We were working harder (changing and setting up machines is a lot more work than keeping them running) at a more skilled level and making less profit!

Our upper management didn't understand the difference in the degree of difficulty between producing specials versus producing stock. Our management felt that the stock plant had better service and was better run than our plant because we received more complaints, which were almost entirely on specials.

In this case, increasing our prices wasn't easy to do as our largest customers were the ones that purchased the specials. We were in a box that was very difficult to get out of and correct the situation. The moral of the story is: Don't get yourself into the box in the first place. Understand the difference between stock and specials and don't get sucked into competing for specials with low prices. Let your competition take low-priced custom products! That is a *no-win situation*. Don't get sucked into playing this game. If your competition's plant is full running low-margin business that means that you can run the good stuff. The lesson is to know what the good stuff is!

The second lesson to be learned from my example is that upper management didn't know the difference between having good technical skills and circumstance. Most upper management assumes that if a business is making a good profit then they are well managed. I have seen more businesses make good money in spite of themselves and their poor practices. The upper management mistook circumstance for good management, and that is dangerous because it can often be just circumstances that are making money for a business. Another one of my rules is: **Just because a business is making a good profit doesn't mean it is well managed or well led.**

To effectively turn a business around, you must understand what drives the profit of your specific business. For example, is it profit per machine hour; is it utilization of capacity because of high fixed costs; is it quick change times; or is it a key patent which insulates your product from price competition?

It is incredible how many managers implement a strategy without knowing their competitive advantage. **You must ask yourself, what is my competitive advantage? What things must I leverage in order to accelerate the growth of my bottom line?**

Too many businesses follow a ready-fire-aim process. Know what you must shoot at before you pull the trigger. Once the toothpaste is out of the tube, you cannot get it back in.

Gross Margin Analysis

There is a second important dimension to pricing that must also be considered. One of the first and most significant things I did to turn around the business in a plant I worked for was to review our gross margins by product and by customer. Gross margin is the amount of profit margin after your material, labor, overhead, and outbound transportation costs.

What I found was shocking. Approximately 25% of our transactions were at single digit or zero margin percent. Approximately 10% of our transactions were at a loss. I called the sales manager in and asked him why this was occurring. He said that corporate management wanted him to increase sales volume and that his own and his sales reps' bonuses were based upon achieving sales unit goals.

The sales department's goals and the true goals of the business were on two different pages. My challenge was to get sales on the same page. From that point on, I spoke with the sales manager often. I convinced him that if we couldn't make a reasonable profit, the plant would close and that we wouldn't have jobs. I convinced him that without a job there would be no bonuses.

At every monthly sales meeting thereafter, each sales rep's results were reviewed in sales dollars, total margin dollars, and in margin percents. Sales bonuses were paid upon achieving their margin dollar targets. The amount of bonus they were paid was based upon a sliding scale of margin dollar results versus their margin dollar targets. A good month was when we exceeded our budgeted margin dollars. Needless to say, we turned the business around. This wasn't the only thing we did. It was, however, the most significant thing we did to turn around the business. We took the business from a 1.9% ROS to a 7.8% ROS in one year! Don't get me wrong, 7.8% ROS isn't really a great result, unless you consider where we were the previous year.

The moral of the story is to make sure that your whole organization's goals and objectives are on the same page. Very often, they are not. **You must personally review your margin results**. One of our sales reps was fixing his own quotations. He was utilizing run speeds and change times that we had never achieved in order to artificially produce lower costs and hit required margin targets on paper. As a result, he was able to exceed his sales margin goals on paper and make a good bonus. Only when I personally reviewed his quotations did I find out what was really happening. If you don't take the time to review the top two lines, sales and cost of sales, in detail to find out what is happening, your chances of successfully turning around the bottom line of a business are slim.

Summary

Here is my rule: **You must personally manage the top two lines in order to improve your bottom line**. No amount of cost cutting, headcount reduction, or counting paper clips could have accomplished what we were able to accomplish by getting our sales and margin goals for the sales force and sales management on the same page as the goals of the business. There are no short cuts. As Stephen Covey said, you must plow the field, plant the seed, fertilize and water the crop before you can expect a harvest. It will take time, effort, and energy. But then, I've already told you that, haven't I?

Chapter Twenty
Workbook

- Why aren't all margin percents equal?

_____

_____

_____

_____

- What is the most important differentiation you need to make when pricing custom versus standard products?

_____

_____

_____

- When evaluating the attractiveness of custom or special, how do you decide which piece of business is more attractive? (Hint: Think about total hours on your machines and margin dollars per machine hour.)

_____

_____

_____

_____

_____

- If your business is making a good profit, how can you evaluate whether or not it is well managed?

_____

_____

_____

_____

_____

_____

- How does your sales rep bonus program directly influence the results of your business?

_____

_____

_____

_____

_____

- What is the best type of goal to establish for your sales reps' bonuses? (Hint: It isn't units.)

_____

_____

_____

_____

• What type of processes might you utilize to get operations and sales on the same page with goals that mutually support bottom-line improvement?

_____

_____

_____

_____

_____

CHAPTER TWENTY-ONE

BUSINESS UNIT SEGMENTATION/ COST ACCOUNTING

One of the most important things you need to do to resuscitate your business is to break it into segments. When you "average" everything together, it is impossible to focus on the right problems and rifle shoot them. Instead, you will end up machine gunning the entire breadth of products and customers, hoping you might hit something.

You cannot find out what is broken if you average everything. The losers get "averaged" in with the winners. As a result, it is impossible to be able to isolate the real problem areas. This whole process is usually called cost accounting, a term that sends many business people scrambling, though it shouldn't. If you don't divide your business into logical segments, it is impossible to really see what is going on within the organization.

So what business segments should you create in your business? The answer is, it depends on your circumstances. There isn't any one correct solution for every business. There are many ways to segment your business. When I worked for GE in one of their television manufacturing divisions very early in my career, I segmented by the two main product lines, color and black and white, and by sales channel within these two product lines. The sales channels were retail, contract, and private label.

By segmenting the business in this fashion, we were able to assess the real potential of the private label business and saw that it made sense incrementally to be in that business segment. As a result, we went from significant losses in the millions of dollars to a small profit in a very short period of time.

In a wholesale or retail business, it is just as important to keep track of sales and costs by product category, department, or product type. Typically, a grid analysis is kept:

- By product category
- By department
- By supplier

For example, in the dairy section of most grocery stores, statistics are kept on the sales and margin of various products but also by brand and additionally by the square footage (shelf space) occupied. In the restaurant industry, table turns by shift are maintained by each store, and gross margins from the bar, dine-in, and carry-out are monitored.

In a business I ran, we segmented it into three separate business units. We chose to segment into long run, short run, and machinery. We found that the long-run segment actually made a percent ROS that was twice as high as the total business. This obviously meant that we had problems in the other two segments. We found that the short-run business was breaking even and that the machinery business was losing money. This enabled us to make much better decisions than if we treated them all as a single, total business.

As a result, we were able to focus on each segment more effectively and make better business decisions. For example, we reduced our manning in the machinery sector to stop the bleeding but didn't touch the manning of the other two segments. We invested $200,000 in a quick-change kit for our short-run printing press in order to lower our change times and increase throughput. We were also able to look at the long-run business and determine that the manufacturing costs for large jobs weren't any-where near as high as we thought they were. For example:

	Blended Costs	Segmented Costs
Materials	$3.50/M	$3.50/M
Labor & O/H	$3.50/M	$2.00/M
Total	$7.00/M	$5.50/M
Selling Price	$10.00/M	$7.85/M
Margin Percent	30%	30%

As a result, we were able to be more price competitive on long-run jobs and grow that segment while maintaining our margin levels. Without segmentation, we would never have been able to be price competitive on big jobs. This is what business unit segmentation can do for you.

The barriers to being able to successfully implement it in most organizations are:

- A lack of talented, experienced business unit managers within the business
- A lack of commitment from corporate to invest into the team building, development, and training necessary to have effective business unit teams
- The unwillingness of the local business management to spend the time necessary to properly evaluate the best business units to segment into
- The unwillingness of the local business management to incur the pain, time effort, and energy needed to implement the business unit segmentation

This tactic is one of the most powerful tools an organization has available. The players in the organization will not normally bring this concept to the general manager/COO/CEO. He or she must be its champion and drive it to completion or it simply won't happen.

What you must recognize and realize is that the number of orders usually drives activity in your business. It takes as much time to spec, quote, enter an order, schedule an order, ship an order, bill an order, and collect an order for $100 as for $1 million. A business with 100 orders a month and $1 million a month in sales will have more labor than a business with 10 orders a month with $1 million a month in sales.

If you have the same overhead rates or machine hour rates for standard products as you have for custom products, you are in trouble. The indirect manufacturing support costs per thousand units are much higher for short-run business. This is because it takes about the same amount of resources and there are fewer units over which to spread the costs.

By utilizing a "blended" rate, you are understating your short-run costs and penalizing your long-run costs. As a result, you will never be as competitive on long-run quotations as you could have been, and your plant will probably be running at less than full capacity. This causes your overhead and support costs per thousand units to be higher and thus lose even more opportunities. It is like a cancer breeding upon itself.

My rule is: **Segment your businesses and your costs. If you don't, you will never achieve your potential!** There isn't a magic formula as to what segments you should utilize for your business. Examples of segments could be:

- Product line or product group
- Retail, contract, or private label
- Long run or short run
- Large customers or small customers
- By technology, for example: electric vs. gas, high rpm vs. low rpm, etc.

One mistake most managers make is to segment by the largest dollar groupings—that is, the segments that are readily apparent and identifiable. Don't fall into this trap! The obvious ones are usually the wrong ones! Why, you ask? The segments that need to be managed independently are beneath the surface. They are segments that are usually impacted by the way the support costs of your business are impacted.

Most financial groupings are being reported by accountants who do not understand the true drivers of cost in your business. They tend to report by segments that are easy to identify, such as products, because they can create sorts on their computers from existing databases.

The right business segmentation must be done by analysis, not by computer sorts and listings. The analysis must be done by legwork and investigation, not by automated programs. The key managers of the business must get involved; don't make the big mistake of entrusting this project to your accountant. One big tip is that indirect support costs are difficult to directly assign. The accountants usually like to "allocate" these types of costs. **Don't let them do it!** Support costs are normally driven by activity. Activity is usually driven by the number of orders.

The easiest way to understand this principal is to imagine what your organization staffing would look like under two different scenarios. Under scenario one, your business has one big customer who gives you one big order on January 1st. You must ship one-twelfth of the total each month on the last day of each month. There are no changes to the specifications.

Under scenario number two, you have one thousand small customers who each give you one hundred small orders per month. The specifications on each order change each month. You cannot pre-build inventory. The quantities vary each month.

Now think in terms of the differences in staffing you would need for activities such as:

- Scheduling
- Order entry
- Purchasing
- Receiving
- Shipping
- Set-up effort and time for each order
- Billing
- Collection
- Material handling
- Customer service

The difference is enormous. This visual picture gives you a good idea of why a lot of the drivers of the costs of your business aren't grouped and reported by your accountants and why they are then hidden from your view.

Even cost accountants, those who specialize in the art of cost allocation and pricing, can have a lot of difficulty pinning the costs to the right product. As a result, in almost *every* environment, there is a good chance that products are costed incorrectly.

Understanding this concept and correctly segmenting your business is one of the most important things you can do. Don't fail to tackle it because it is foreign to you and it is difficult to do. Do not fail to do it because it is the realm of the accountants. Do not be put off by the many assumptions and different approaches that are necessary to make it successful.

Knowing your cost structure will enable you to correctly cost, price, and quote your products and services. If you are not doing this accurately, it may be part of the reason why your business is losing money.

Summary

Cost accounting and accounting for business segments is a difficult, time-consuming process. Whether you like it or not, it is one of those steps that is essential for success. If it is not done correctly, you could be selling your products at a loss and not even realize it. If done with dedication and accuracy, it could be the boost you need to make your business successful.

Chapter Twenty-One
Workbook

- What are the key reasons why you should segment your business into separate units?

  _____

  _____

  _____

  _____

- What are the barriers preventing you from using business unit segmentation in your organization? How can you overcome them?

  _____

  _____

  _____

  _____

- How do the number of orders you receive impact the cost levels of your organization?

  _____

  _____

  _____

  _____

- What types of indirect costs are impacted by the number of orders you receive?

_____

_____

_____

_____

_____

CHAPTER TWENTY-TWO

SCHEDULING

I took a deep breath before I started this chapter because I could have written a book on this subject. Just about every failing business I've seen up close and personal has had serious problems with scheduling their plant.

I have seen a manufacturing plant have two-thirds of their orders in house on the hot list to be expedited. How can they possibly be cost effective or reliably scheduling this way? I've had plants put a 25% cushion in their lead times and wonder why they didn't have enough business. I've had plants that felt that their performance was outstanding not know that 33% of their orders were consistently late.

Scheduling problems are just as rampant in the service sector as well. How many times have you been to a store that was empty of customers but staffed to the limit with people who had nothing to do? How about the restaurant that operates all day long even though 80% of their business is at dinner? Scheduling is a problem no matter what kind of business.

The bad news is that there aren't any easy answers here. The good news is that there are some guidelines and principles that can be utilized.

The first thing you have to decide is what kind of business you are in. That is, do you need to schedule your business to optimize your efficiency and lower your costs or do you need to schedule your plant to meet your customers' whims? While a lot of businesses adopt an either/or approach to scheduling, there are some things you can do to accomplish some of both.

Scheduling for Service Sector Enterprises

The most important issue in staffing a service enterprise is the dynamics of the customer service process. If your business is relatively constant, the only issue is the efficiency of the staffing. When your business is a retail business, where there are issues of whether to be open or not, it is much more difficult. You have got to balance cost against customer service, remaining open at odd hours versus the revenue gained by longer hours.

The level of staffing in most service industries is not a clear-cut analysis. How many times have you had to wait in long lines at a store or stay on hold for an unacceptable time, all because some manager made the decision to run "lean"? The problem with running too lean is that there is no way to objectively evaluate what the limit is of running understaffed. Obviously, if potential customers are leaving the store without buying, sales are being lost. On the other hand, what happens when sales appear to go up but observation shows long lines? It may be that additional customers are not willing to stand in long lines.

With a call center operation, it is very easy to assess the wait times for calls. Sometimes, managers try to use "average" wait times to justify running lean. Is this a fair measurement? If there is no wait for 15 hours, less than five minutes for seven hours, and 45 minutes for the peak times, is a 24-hour average really useful? Probably, it is not. Another statistic, easily attainable from the phone company, is the number of busy signals on the company's phone lines. While not specifically related to staffing, an excess number of busy signals indicates that potential customers are having a hard time getting through to the company. The staffing may be acceptable for the number of lines; there just may not be enough lines!

The most difficult analyses are those for businesses with highly seasonal workforce requirements. Resorts, retail outlets, CPAs, and other such businesses have a difficult time staffing. Balancing the need to have trained staff on hand when needed versus the "dead time" overhead is a challenge. Obviously, the solution is to find some off-season complementary activity. Resorts have moved to hosting conventions and meetings. CPAs have expanded into financial advisory services, and lawn care companies do spring and fall cleanup as well as snow removal.

The bottom line on scheduling is to have enough manpower to meet your demand. Pricing your product to pay for some excess supply of labor is one good way to ensure quality customer service.

Scheduling for Manufacturing

First of all, you need to segment your production between standard products and custom products to a specification. Standard products are normally made for inventory. These must be scheduled in the most cost effective, productive manner. How do you do that?

First of all, don't mix your custom and standard products' production on the same machines. Segment them. Custom products normally require long set-up times and are generally shorter runs than standard products. If you are mixing the production of both types on the same production equipment, you will make the custom products late and the standard products artificially more expensive.

How can that be? Your accounting people won't be able to segment the run times, set-up times, and waste by product group on the same production equipment. As a result, your additional production costs associated with custom products will get "allocated" to your standard products and make them non-competitive. Your standard product production will generally make the deliveries of your custom products late because you cannot adequately predict inventory turnover rates by individual production machine when you are quoting the delivery dates for your custom-made product.

The solution is to segment the two by individual production machine(s). If you are manufacturing custom-made products only, segment your scheduling by individual machine between long and short runs. Otherwise, the change times of your short-run business will get in the way of the timely delivery of your long runs. The collective additional change times of your short runs on a machine will also artificially raise the cost of your long-run products because your accountants won't be able to differentiate the change time costs between product groups on the same production machine.

By mixing long and short runs of custom products or mixing standard products with custom products on the same production equipment, you get the worst of both worlds. The worst results are high standard product costs and poor on-time deliveries on custom products. The normal solution to this predicament is overtime and more costs.

In short, the "damned if you do and damned if you don't" and "it is due tomorrow" type of environment is usually a result of a system problem and not poor effort. In a nutshell, the problem is management, not the production workers.

I am absolutely amazed by how many manufacturing plants that are making custom products do not track and report their on-time delivery rates. One reason for this is that they don't want management to know how bad the situation really is. If you are manufacturing custom products that have specific due dates and you are not tracking your percent of on-time deliveries, trust me when I say that you are already in hot water!

One of the most important principles to follow in scheduling is to set realistic delivery lead times and quote delivery dates utilizing these times. It is far better to lose an order than it is to lose a customer. You should always allow one day every two weeks or so for break-in emergency orders. In addition, you should never utilize Saturdays as part of your quoted lead times unless you are working every Saturday. Use Saturday to lower your lead times, bail out jobs that are running late, and for hot break-in jobs. Once you start counting on Saturday to determine your quoted delivery dates, you lose your flexibility and your ability to catch up if you are behind.

One word of caution: A favorite trick of many manufacturing floor supervisors to artificially improve their on-time delivery performance is the revised due date. When they realize that they will be late, they simply call the customer and notify them of the fact. They then enter the new, revised ship date and then track their on-time delivery performance against the revised date.

The point here is that even if they hit the revised ship date, **it is still late!** Track your on-time performance against the original date unless your customer requires a change to the product specification or quantity. If they make a change, then it is perfectly all right to track delivery performance to the revised ship date.

The other benefit of scheduling your plant separately between custom and standard products or between long and short run is that you will increase your capacity! How can that be, you ask? By running standard or custom and long-run or short-run products on the same equipment, you have to "average" your manning resources. In other words, you man your machines for the total annual or average output. As a result, they are understaffed for the changes required with custom and multiple short-run jobs and overstaffed for standard and long-run jobs.

By segmenting the machines on which you run custom and short-run products, you can more effectively differentiate your manning. If, for example, you have four people a shift on your printing presses, you normally deploy two per press. By differentiating and running custom or short-run products on one press you can also differentiate your manning. Both custom and short-run products produce more change times and longer change times.

You must deploy your staffing to address your change time requirements! You can and should deploy three people to the custom or short-run equipment and one person to the standard or long-run product equipment. **The result will be less change time, longer run times, and more production!**

Summary

Scheduling is an important issue with which many failing businesses face problems. No matter what business you are in, staffing can cause issues that affect your bottom line. You obviously want to schedule so as to be most cost effective and productive, but this is not always as simplistic as it sounds and may require a great deal of balancing. Each business requires its own analyses, for staffing is an area that you must monitor and track accurately or face negative consequences.

Chapter Twenty-Two
Workbook

- Why do you need to segment the products you produce in order to achieve effective scheduling?

_____

_____

_____

_____

_____

- Why do you need to dedicate your production equipment to your product segments?

_____

_____

_____

_____

- Do you continuously know what your on-time delivery performance is for your product segments?

_____

_____

_____

_____

- Are you actively managing your scheduling or are you reacting to each daily crisis and the irate customer of the day? If it is the latter, what can you do about it? What positive changes could you make to improve your approach?

_____

_____

_____

_____

_____

CHAPTER TWENTY-THREE

QUALITY

This chapter will probably seem a little strange to you. So many companies are going to a version of ISO 9000. Now, ISO 9000, 9001, or 9002 can improve your quality. There is no guarantee, however, that it will. It takes an enormous amount of time, effort, and resources to get qualified. In a turnaround situation, you don't have time or the resources to utilize ISO.

Don't despair; there is another way to do it! You must start from the point of view that quality is free. That is, whatever amount of reasonable time and money you spend on it, it will end up saving you money. If you don't already understand this, then you must go to some seminars or pick up some W. Edwards Deming books.

It is amazing to me how many plants still have quality control departments and try to inspect quality at the end. In other words, they pay attention to quality by inspecting things as they are finished. That's backwards! Quality begins at the first step of the production process, not at the end.

A simple analogy will prove the point. If a store owner buys porcelain vases and puts everything that the manufacturer sends on display without any inspection, what will the store look like? Customers will see some defective merchandise, some broken units, and some vases with missing lids, etc. all displayed together. The customer will have to figure out which units are free from defect. What impression will the customer have? The store owner should inspect each unit as it is received. Defective units should be isolated and sent back for credit. The customer should only see the highest quality unit.

So it is in a manufacturing environment. The job of quality begins at the receiving dock when materials are received. Each stage of manufacturing requires quality checks. It starts with your staff. You must personally make sure that your workers are building quality. How do you do that? Go out on the floor and talk to them. Ask them how they know whether or not they are making good quality products. Ask them to show you how they check their quality.

Examine their quality-checking instruments. If quality is an issue for your business, and in most failing businesses it is, then you must personally tackle this issue. You cannot initially expect your plant manager and supervisors to do it for you. The truth is that if they knew how to do it, they would have already done it. They can be taught, and they can learn, but you do not have two years; you must turn your quality around in six months.

I went to lunch one day with one of my supervisors. This is after we had already made a dramatic improvement in our quality. My boss had run this business for six months prior to my taking over the operation. This supervisor asked me why my boss or the previous general manager hadn't fixed the quality problem. It dawned on me that a really good supervisor didn't realize that when important issues like quality don't get fixed, it is usually because the managers don't know how to fix it.

The best way to determine whether or not you have high quality is to talk to your customers. While you should always check your returns and credits as a percent of sales, not all quality problems show up as returns and credits. Customers will usually tell you what they think. You must, however, get out and get in front of them. Getting this information on the phone is almost impossible.

The other way to obtain feedback is to track credits for bad quality as a percent of sales. If you're making standard products, then your credits should not be more than 0.2% of sales. While this certainly isn't world class, it will usually keep you out of trouble. If you are making custom products to individual specifications, your credits shouldn't exceed 0.5% of sales. This percentage is also not world class but likewise should keep you out of trouble.

So how do you achieve good quality? For starters, you must have:

- Written procedures and practices that are clearly communicated, understood, and enforced

- Extensive training so that employees know what good quality looks like and how to spot rejects

- Empowered employees who will stop the process and fix the problem

- Well-maintained equipment that can hold tolerances

- Quality materials that can perform the required application(s)

- Written specifications on key characteristics with which employees can accurately measure product variability

- Accountability — employees are held accountable for producing good quality

- Active and highly visible top management support for the cause

- Quality goals that are well communicated

- Quantifiable measurements of quality and timely reporting of results versus goals

In order to implement all these things, you must personally drive it yourself. There are no substitutes. Don't make the mistake of thinking that you can delegate this responsibility. The truth is that it will take a minimum of three months to implement it, six months until you start seeing results, and twelve months to discipline and/or fire employees who won't or can't meet expectations.

If you have the above conditions, you will most likely achieve high quality without an ISO 9000 program. You can achieve good results in six months if you work hard at it and utilize the above principles. In one plant, we cut credits from 2.3% of sales to 0.8% in six months. In another plant, we lowered credits from 0.6% of sales to 0.26% in a little more than a year. In fact, the last job was more difficult because it was making custom products, and 0.6% credits as a percent of sales wasn't out of control in the first place.

None of the principles are easy to implement, but they are certainly easier than ISO 9000. Of these principles, the principle of accountability is probably the hardest but also the most important. It is the hardest because you must have manufacturing supervision that will hold employees accountable and work with them to improve performance. In every one of my turnaround situations, we had to let at least one employee go because of repeated bad quality. If you don't discipline people who have been retrained and are still making bad quality, you will never solve the problem.

One critical action you must take to improve quality is to demand COAs (certificates of analysis) from your suppliers. This certifies that your raw materials are in specification. Be careful here, however, because there are specifications and then there are specifications! What I mean is that specifications are only as good as the range or tolerances. If the tolerances are set so far apart that you can drive an 18-wheeler through without touching the sides, then you can bet you are getting shoddy product.

How can you find out if this scenario is happening? Ask for a graph of your actual product specifications for the past six months, including the current shipment, before you actually receive the material. Visually look at the variance of the current shipment versus what you have been getting that you know works. If, for example, you are receiving a shipment of ink and the viscosity is 34.5 seconds (on a zion cup), and the upper limit is 35.0 seconds, you should accept it, right? Not necessarily! If the ink you have been using for the past six months has been running in the 24.0 to 26.0 second range, **Houston, we have a problem!** Reject it! Don't even let it in the door! The fact is that most manufacturers set their upper and lower specification limits for their own convenience. They do not want customers to reject product but rather to accept it when their manufacturing processes vary! **Don't let them do this to you!**

Another one of my rules is: **Making good quality is a reflection of management's attitude about it.** You personally must set the tone and the expectation. In all four of the turnarounds that I have had to engineer, quality was a major issue. To improve, you will have to educate everyone, discipline some people, and, regrettably, let some people go.

If you do not personally emphasize quality, then the organization won't consider it to be a top priority. You preach it, and you must drive it. You effectively drive it in your organization by making sure good goals and objectives are set but also by measuring quality very closely and very often. You make sure it is in your bonus plans and in your managers' and supervisors' performance appraisals. Measure it closely and often, and it will improve.

Put new practices in place and make sure your people follow the new practices. Hold people accountable and discipline them for repeated bad quality. Impact your bonus payments, performance reviews, and salary increases for good quality. These practices will all help you to improve quality.

It doesn't take some international standards organization like ISO 9000 to make good quality. Talking about quality is good, but it will not happen as a result of that alone. It does, however, take commitment, focus, effort, goals, measurements, accountability, discipline, and financial rewards. Remember, I told you that turnarounds aren't for the faint of heart. Don't expect to be popular.

Summary

Quality, or the lack of it, can drive your company's success or failure in the marketplace. Whether you run a CPA firm, own a hair salon, manufacture widgets, or build fighter jets, the principles are the same. It starts with commitment, it becomes part of every process in the delivery of goods and services, and it pervades the entire attitude of the company. When your company has a fanatic dedication to quality, it is hard to avoid being successful.

Chapter Twenty-Three
Workbook

• If you are in a turnaround situation and your business isn't ISO qualified, why shouldn't you spend the time and effort to get qualified immediately?

_____

_____

_____

_____

• What is the quickest and most effective way to find out how good or bad your quality is? Why is this the best way?

_____

_____

_____

_____

• If you need to improve your quality quickly, how do you go about achieving that goal?

_____

_____

_____

_____

_____

- Do you require COAs from your key suppliers? If you do not, why not? If so, what do these reports show you?

_____

_____

_____

_____

_____

- Why is it important to get a graphic portrayal of the actual specifications of your key materials? What can it tell you?

_____

_____

_____

_____

_____

CHAPTER TWENTY-FOUR

NEW BUSINESS DEVELOPMENT

In every one of the turnaround situations that I have faced, the need for more sales was the single greatest issue. Of course, there was a bushel basket full of reasons causing this problem.

The purpose of this chapter isn't to go back over how to fix a lot of the causes. The purpose is to stimulate new thinking about how to generate new business or more sales.

Price

Price is the easy vehicle. How many businesses have gone bankrupt trying to increase sales by being the price leader? If all you do to get more volume is cut pricing, you won't be successful. Sure, you must be price competitive. The place to start, however, is to know your costs.

In order to know your costs, you have to segment your businesses and not "blend" costs of goods sold and overhead costs. By segmenting your costs, you can be more competitive when you need to be. In fact, the whole issue of setting price relies upon your ability to understand costs. Unfortunately, this is one area of the business where the bean counters and the marketing staff must work together.

If you do not really know your costs under varying levels of sales and output, playing with prices can be a disaster. Despite what common sense might tell you, what a product actually costs out the door with all the costs of after-sale support factored in may be completely different from what you suppose.

Quality

If you are not producing good quality, you had better be the industry's low-cost producer. If your quality is not leading the industry, your costs had better be based on your prices or a very strong patent is going to have to be your main tactic.

Service

Almost all customers want good service. The truth is, unfortunately, that they will rarely pay you a premium for it. They will leave you for another supplier, however. So obviously, you need to find a balance. What is the way to ensure that you have good service? Again, talk to your customers.

Thinking Outside the Envelope

This is the most difficult approach because the opportunities aren't readily apparent. Yet, I have found it to be the most effective. The best way to manage your two top lines, sales and cost of sales, is to think outside of the envelope. Rather than tell you what this means, let me give you some examples.

 I was responsible for running a tissue business for a paper company. The paper machine was more than thirty years old and too narrow and slow to be cost effective making facial and bathroom tissue. We transformed the business into a specialty tissue business. We put in a dye system and a computerized color matching system. We started making deep tone party napkins for Hallmark, poultry wadding for grocery stores, customized tissue for medical applications, and so on. We increased our income by 73% in one year, achieving a 26% return on net assets. Now that's thinking outside the envelope!

I was on board about 30 days when we lost our largest customer for a variety of reasons. We didn't have enough business left to be profitable, no matter how many people we cut. Cutting prices to gain business through our distributors would result in our competition responding in kind. We had to find new opportunities quickly.

We bid a government GSA contract and procured $2 million of new business, which would have caused a pricing war if we had done that in the distributor marketplace. We secured more than $1 million of new business through a large broker. This business wouldn't disrupt our regular distributor sales channel. In both cases, we went through new and different distribution channels to secure new business. If growth in your current channel is about exhausted, instead of plowing the same old field, go mine another field.

 In another business, we were selling stretch sleeve labels. No matter how attractive our pricing, quality, or service was for the labels, the cost of the application equipment was a barrier. While we continued to search for new opportunities, we also decided to get into shrink sleeve labels. This market segment of sleeves was growing at a tremendous rate. We migrated into another segment of the same product. We didn't change our scope; we changed the breadth of our product line. Again, this is thinking outside the envelope.

The bottom line is that to develop new sales, you are going to have to do things that you have not done before. You are going to have to:

- Change your channel of distribution
- Expand and reposition your product line
- Make strategic acquisitions
- Decrease your product line, emphasizing strengths and catering to a specialty market

The fundamental issue is deciding what business you are in and then pursuing the opportunities within that business framework. The problem occurs when a business doesn't properly define itself or locks itself into a business with static markets, declining demand, or against much stronger, bigger competitors.

In order to succeed, a business must have a demonstrable "comparative advantage" in a marketplace that is growing. That is why we just focused on "vision." Changing a vision often requires a complete overhaul of the company's position, structure, product line, and attitude. For a while, that may cause the "fish out of water" syndrome. If done without careful planning and research, the greener pastures may be pure illusion.

All of these things will help your business to grow. The key, however, is really assessing your current situation first and deciding what needs to be done. If you have a cancer within your organization, it must be fixed first in order to branch out successfully.

If, for example, not holding your people accountable for results was an issue in your organization, why would you believe that if you made an acquisition that the same cancer wouldn't spread to the new organization? You must fundamentally fix the root causes of your problems first before you can go plow other fields. The new field offers opportunity, but if your plow isn't functioning properly in your field, chances are it won't work in the new field either. All you will end up with is more unplowed ground that hasn't been properly seeded and fertilized.

Summary

Generating new business is going to require that you think beyond the ordinary and the tested. Many factors go into creating sales, such as price, quality, and service. However, before you can truly grow, you must have assessed just what problems there are in the organization. These issues will have to be corrected first. Ultimately, you must be very focused to improve your sales, focused on your market and your definition of your organization. Here again, a strong vision is required.

Chapter Twenty-Four
Workbook

- What are the major reasons why you don't have more business?

_____

_____

_____

_____

_____

- Have you addressed the above reasons? Have you noted improvements? If not, why do you expect to increase your volume?

_____

_____

_____

_____

_____

- What avenues are open to you to "mine another field"?

_____

_____

_____

_____

_____

CHAPTER TWENTY-FIVE
MARKETING AND SALES

Marketing

We could talk about how to promote your product in this chapter, but promoting your product isn't unique to a turnaround situation. I'm going to talk about how to market in a turnaround situation. You can utilize this approach in other business environments as well.

The most common flaw of failing businesses is not identifying a competitive advantage or simply not having one. Let's talk first about what a competitive advantage is.

Brent Halsey, CEO of James River Paper Company when I worked there, would always grill us on competitive advantage. He wanted to know how we planned on beating our competition before he would buy into a long-range plan. Not only did he want to know about your competitive advantage, he also wanted to know about your competition. This analysis is critical to success, yet most failing businesses have never even thought about it.

A competitive advantage can be several things, such as:

- Low-cost producer
- A patent
- Technology and know-how
- Quality
- Service
- Brand name/Image
- Distribution
- Geographic coverage
- Customer relationships

The first and foremost key to being able to beat your competition is to know what your competitive advantage is. Unless you can identify one, why do you think you can be successful? Even if you have one or more, unless you know what they are, how can you leverage them in the marketplace? Your entire organization must know what your advantages are. Unless they do, how can you effectively leverage them much less maintain them?

Marketing your advantage doesn't necessarily mean brochures, pamphlets, and trade advertisements. Of course, you can utilize these things. The key to successfully marketing your competitive advantage is having your sales and customer service reps effectively execute your advantage every day. If it is, for example, service, they must not only be aware of it, but they must live and breathe it during their contact with customers.

How you manage and motivate them to maintain your competitive advantage of service will determine how long you keep it and how effective it will be. The same holds true for advantages such as quality, being the low-cost producer, and customer relationships. In order to maintain your competitive advantage, you must work at it very hard day in and day out. You must focus on it as well as put financial and human resources into developing and maintaining it.

When you try to turn around a business, too many times you can get sucked into fire fighting. There will be more fires than you can possibly put out. It does no good to simply put out fires if you do not have or cannot develop a significant competitive advantage. The competitive advantage is the deal breaker. That is, if you don't have one or cannot develop one quickly, then it is time to throw in the towel.

Some examples of when throwing in the towel is probably a good idea follow.

We were manufacturing and selling paper products through paper distributors. We didn't have national geographic manufacturing coverage with our plants. Without it, it was impossible to develop effective national contracts with national paper distributors. Without being certified by national paper distributors, we had to deal with regional paper distributors. More and more regional paper distributors were purchased by national companies such as International Paper and XPEDX. We couldn't compete simply because we couldn't secure national distribution coverage. It was a downward spiral, which couldn't be reversed.

 We were a converting division of a national paper company. Being a paper converter, we competed with other customers to whom the paper sales force sold. The paper sales force saw us as a problem and a thorn in their side. How could they sell paper to converters when their company was competing with them? They wanted us out. Since they were significantly bigger and more profitable than us, guess who won? Again, be realistic about the battles you fight. There was no winning this one.

 I started a disposable medical products business for a division of a company making the base fabric my products utilized. The strategy was forward vertical integration, and we would be the low-cost producer. The strategy was sound, except for the fact that the management of the core fabric business didn't want to sell to us as they had to transfer fabric at cost. They not only didn't want to help us, they went out of their way to torpedo us even though we were both part of the same division. Eventually the fabric division was sold to a company that didn't want to manufacture disposable medical products. We ended up having to shut down our business.

These examples should help you to be aware that being successful is more than having good products and good people. Not only must you have a strong competitive advantage, but you must also have the support of your upper management. Life is simply too short, and companies will use you until it isn't to their advantage to do so. Take control of your future. Don't be a martyr and go down with the ship. This doesn't do the business or your career any good. If the turnaround is strategically impossible, don't try and bail water with a bucket that has a three-foot hole in it.

The bottom line is that many average companies with average products can be extraordinarily successful if they market those products effectively. Conversely, many very well-designed, quality products can fail for lack of effecttive marketing

Think competitive advantage at each stage of the marketing plan. Identify potential clients and customers and see the sale from their perspective. What perceived benefits do they receive from dealing with your company instead of the competition? Find them, focus on them, and grow your sales.

Sales Management

We have already talked about how to develop new business and get more sales. I gave you some different ideas on how to do this. Now, I am going to give you the basic blocking and tackling example on how to grow your sales.

In looking back at the four businesses I have turned around, three of the four weren't properly executing basic and effective sales management. That means, in plain language, that they weren't managing the sales function very well. The good news here is that it isn't rocket science. The bad news is that poor sales management is so prevalent that it is inexplicable.

What should you look for? Plenty! The first thing you must do is develop a system to keep track of how many calls the sales staff is making. It blew me away to see how much time sales reps in failing businesses spent in the office. It is so prevalent that it is an epidemic! You must set sales call targets for your sales reps, and you must, I repeat, you must, keep score.

If you only target the number of sales calls, what usually happens is that they will call on the customers they like the most and with whom they feel comfortable. You must also make a second and very important distinction, which is to target and monitor the amount of new business your sales reps are generating. Simply calling on the existing base of business, while it will help you defend what you already have, will seldom help you grow your sales at a high rate.

The basic premise here is that in order to rapidly grow your sales, you must bring in new business. Just what is new business? That is up to you to define. In general, it means that you have secured some new sales that you didn't previously have. It can be a new customer, a new plant or production line with an existing customer, or an additional product sale at an existing customer that you previously didn't have.

Again, you must differentiate and track new business by individual sales representatives. You must make sure that each and every sales rep is spending a significant amount of their time (at least 40%) calling on new customers or new buying influences within existing customers.

You must offer your sales reps an incentive to develop new business because new business is harder to generate and takes more effort to accomplish. Sales reps have to do the pick-and-shovel work of prospecting. They have to get by protective administrative assistants; they have to leave numerous voice mail messages as most key decision makers don't directly answer their phones. This activity sucks up time, and time is money. It is a lot easier to call a "friend" and ask for the order. Only a few sales reps will willingly take on this chore without a strong financial incentive — so, give them one!

There is one additional thing that you must do. You must make generating new business a job requirement. The lack of new business development must be a performance issue. It cannot be optional with the only consequence being bonuses or commissions.

You have to have a sales manager who manages. That implies leading, training, developing, and monitoring sales activities. It necessitates thinking outside of the box. It involves doing things to create new opportunities. A good sales manager will orchestrate a campaign involving sales calls, mailings, telemarketing, trade shows, print advertising, and will work closely with the marketing manager to assure that the lowest cost per dollar sales is achieved.

The sales manager should keep statistics of all sales campaigns and their relative success. Statistics on individuals on the sales staff must also be maintained. Some organizations use activity-based compensation systems, while others use sales only. It is probably better to combine the two or have a small base salary plus commission on the gross margin generated.

Most sales organizations leave the actual sales presentation to the sales person to develop and implement. That is an incredibly inefficient, hit-or-miss proposition. On the other hand, a straight jacketed presentation that has been memorized won't do anyone any good.

The statistics on the average sales call cost for an industrial company comes to something more than $100 per call. At that rate, some efficiencies and maximum effectiveness had better be there or a lot of money will be wasted.

Far too many companies fail to grasp the importance of combining efficiency plus effectiveness. For example, a typical sales cycle might look like this:

1. Mail
2. Telemarket
3. Visit
4. Visit
5. Visit and bid
6. Follow-up visit
7. Re-bid
8. Follow-up visit
9. Close

Is that an efficient way to market? Perhaps the process could be simplified:

1. Mail
2. Telemarket
3. Send video
4. Telemarket — gather bidding facts
5. Visit and bid
6. Follow up by phone
7. Close

One step has been eliminated, and another has been replaced with a much cheaper but perhaps more efficient alternative. The total cost savings could amount to several hundred dollars per sales, allow greater sales staff productivity, and result in a higher close ratio.

Continual sales training is imperative. The sales staff needs constant reaffirmation, esprit de corps building and reinforcement of their sales skills. Seminars, in-house training sessions, role playing, and presentation by the sales staff should be part of weekly sales training meetings. If you find a situation in which weekly meetings are not being held, or training is not occurring regularly, you have a problem. The sales manager should be constantly looking for new ways to improve the efficiency and effectiveness of the staff. If you find a situation in which the sales manager is content doing the same old thing, you probably have a problem.

The other key issue to growing your sales is having a competitive edge. This competitive edge can be one of many things such as:

- Being the low-cost producer
- Efficiency supremacy
- Patents
- Service
- Quality
- Delivery lead times
- On-time deliveries
- Flexibility to respond to customer emergencies
- Key relationships
- All of the above

Now having a competitive edge doesn't do you any good unless your sales force understands what it is. You must drill your competitive edge into your sales force so that they know it better than their social security number.

Secondly, your sales force must know how to leverage your competitive edge into securing a sale. Having a competitive edge does you no good unless your sales reps know how to use it to secure the order against their competition.

If your competitive advantage is quality, they must have hard statistics and great references from existing customers in order to create a competitive edge. Telling your customer, for example, that you are ISO 9000 certified doesn't create a competitive edge. Telling your customer, for example, that your failure rate is one hundredth of one percent and showing them the hard data to back it up is a whole different story. Asking them about their current supplier's failure rate is a way to leverage your competitive edge to get an order.

Summary

To successfully market your product in a turnaround situation, you must focus on your competitive advantage. The entire organization must know not only what the advantage is but also concentrate on it every day at all times; it should be their primary objective. Without it, your company will not survive. Marketing your advantage will require an efficient, well-managed sales staff that receives on-going training and skills development.

Chapter Twenty-Five
Workbook

- What are your competitive advantages?

_____

_____

_____

_____

- Does your organization know what your advantages are? How do you communicate them to workers?

_____

_____

_____

_____

- How are you effectively leveraging your advantages in the marketplace?

_____

_____

_____

_____

- What is the single most important strategic factor you need to be able to turn a business around?

_____

_____

_____

- Do you have this strategic factor? If not, what do you intend to do about it?

_____

_____

_____

_____

- Are you effectively tracking the frequency and quality of the sales calls your sales reps are making? Do you have a written targeted number of sales calls per month?

_____

_____

_____

- Do you have written goals for new business for your sales reps? Are you tracking the amount of new business your sales force generates each month?

_____

_____

_____

- What incentive are you offering your sales force to develop new business?

_____

_____

_____

_____

_____

CHAPTER TWENTY-SIX

CONCLUSION

We will finish our discussion where we started — with leadership. I have already defined and described it for you. I will now attempt to give you a profile of the type of leadership you will need to turn a business around. Thomas Peters and Robert Waterman wrote about "management by wandering around" in their book *In Search of Excellence.* Managing by wandering around means that management literally gets out into the business, talks to employees, and finds out what is truly happening in the workplace. It is a means of gathering employee feedback.

To be effective, you must do more than just wander around. Simply talking to people is not proactive or participative enough. You must personally get involved. What then is the difference between wandering around and getting involved?

- Wandering around means observing up close and personal what is happening. It means listening to your people's concerns, issues, and needs.

- Getting involved means more than just listening and observing. It means personally being part of the solution. It means making sure that the issue gets addressed by being part of the team that addresses it or by meeting with the team to monitor their progress while they address the issue.

Hands-on managers combine these two ideas. They gain feedback from all levels of an organization, and then they utilize this information to institute change. If you are out on the floor one day a month, you will not likely get accurate, useful information from people. If you do not use the information that you obtain, people will probably stop sharing with you. You must observe and talk to people, and you must use the information you gain to create solutions to problems. By combining the two principles and executing them sincerely and regularly, you will be a more effective leader and produce improvements within the organization.

To engineer a turnaround, you must be a hands-on manager. Forget about strictly delegating and hoping that things will get done. Even with good people, problems in an organization that is failing usually don't get solved unless you are personally involved. You cannot engineer a turnaround from behind your desk. You can plan one from there, but you cannot drive one from there. The message is that you must personally *drive* a turnaround. I'm *not* saying that you have to do everything yourself. You cannot. However, you must determine which things are critical and then get personally involved in them to ensure that they get done right and get done in a timely manner.

Getting involved doesn't mean you do it all yourself. It means that you participate in the team meetings (if you don't have a team on the project, you are probably already in trouble). It means that you ensure that progress is being made at a significantly effective rate. It means removing obstacles, helping make difficult decisions in a timely fashion, supplying adequate resources, having an established timeline, and tracking progress against it.

You can only get involved in so many of these projects, so you must prioritize. Setting the priorities is one of the most important things a leader can do in a turnaround situation. Helping drive the program is critical. You shouldn't be the project leader, but you must be an active team participant.

If your style is to read reports and ask occasional questions, you might as well pack it in early. If your style is to delegate the important things that must get done and assume they will be taken care of, you had better update your resume. Remember that delegation without supervision and accountability is abdication. Delegate, yes, delegate extensively but ensure that those to whom you delegate report back to you on a regular basis regarding the progress of their projects and that you hold them accountable for their commitments.

Having to get involved and personally drive the important priorities is why engineering a turnaround is so physically and mentally demanding. Engineering a turnaround requires twice as much energy as running a successful business does. Trust me, I'm not exaggerating.

Now, here is the *key dichotomy*. While you must be involved in driving programs to their timely conclusion, you cannot be autocratic in doing so. This means that you don't call all the shots, not even most of them. You might have to make a few critical decisions on your own. If you make most of them, however, it becomes your project and team members will lose interest, energy, and commitment.

You must be more of a facilitator than the project team leader. Your main function is to:

- Keep projects and priorities on schedule.
- Make sure the key objectives are being met.
- Keep the team from falling off the edge of a cliff, crashing, and burning.
- Ensure team harmony and make sure that nobody is monopolizing the decision making or the agenda, including *you.*
- Make sure that everyone is contributing and that conflict isn't being avoided or creating gridlock.
- Keep the morale up and the team focused.

This sounds a lot like maintaining control. In some ways it is. In fact, in order to gain control, you must relinquish it. What I mean is that you gain the most effective results from commitment, not control. To gain commitment, you must allow your troops to participate in decision making as well as disagreeing with you. You must give them recognition and encouragement. You must also address team members who aren't pulling their own weight.

You must exhibit a passion for the urgency and importance of the project. You must convince the team working on the project of its importance and how they will, as a group, determine the outcome.

The balancing act between being involved and being participative is an art form. How do you know when you are keeping the two in balance? You must have at least two teammates with whom you can share confidences. Ask them for feedback. Make the effort to see how they see you and how the rest of the staff views you. Nobody can see himself or herself as others do, and what counts the most is how others see you. You *must* ask in order to gain this information.

One word of preparation: Be prepared for some uncomfortable feedback. If everything you receive is glowing, you are either a "water walker" or getting a bunch of feedback that is watered down. It is only through candid feedback that you can hone your skills and achieve the kind of balance that will enable you to achieve the results your business so desperately needs.

The fact is that the upper management in most of the organizations that I have worked for have a management style that is considerably different than that of a participative manager. They tend to manage by either fear and intimidation or by being autocratic. This management style is not only virtually useless in turnaround situations, but it is actually counterproductive.

Why then don't more leaders lead in a participative style? I discussed that issue with Peter Tourtellot, President of the Turnaround Management Association. He indicated that there is usually a common thread that contributes to businesses ending up in a crisis. He said, "There is a common thread that goes back from a lack of communication with employees and customers to not being able to delegate, wanting to do it all yourself, and eventually the whole place caves in because you can't. As the company gets further and further into trouble, managers develop a foxhole mentality; they jump in the foxhole, cover themselves up, and hope nobody can find them. It's called denial."

Tourtellot also said, "The next common thread is [thinking] that the next sale will get me out of trouble. And of course, it doesn't."

None of these reasons are good reasons. They prevent leaders from accomplishing the very difficult task of turning a business around. The vast majority of managers I've worked for or worked under do not manage in a participative manner. They have all been very successful. Yet, few of them can successfully engineer a turnaround because of their management and leadership style.

These managers go with what got them where they are and think that what has made them successful will work in all situations. They get into a complacent mindset and stop attempting to grow and develop their skills. While this can and does work in organizations that do not have as critical of a timeline, it simply cannot and does not work in turnaround situations. Leaders who do not look for feedback on their own performances and who do not view their development as a lifelong process become stagnant. This stagnation at the upper level will eventually affect the entire organization. In a turnaround, change is absolutely necessary at all levels, and this type of stagnation is disastrous.

Why don't good, experienced managers understand this principle? The answer is that most managers have never had to personally turn a business around. As a result, they don't understand that special circumstances require special techniques. They go with what they are comfortable with and think that it will be enough because it got them through in the past.

Resuscitating a dying business isn't about being comfortable. It is about doing the uncomfortable things necessary to save the sinking ship. This is why it is so hard to do. The first instinct of a manager who has been previously successful and who is facing a turnaround situation for the first time is to take charge and take no prisoners. Now, I'm not saying that you don't have to be demanding. If you don't gain the support of the organization to implement fundamental change, which flies in the face of what they have been doing, then forget it. You cannot do it yourself. This is why an autocratic leadership style simply doesn't work in a turnaround situation.

The good news is that a participative management style coupled with intense involvement can be learned. Most people, including myself, were not born with it. I have had to develop it. Yes, I made mistakes along the way. Most managers don't want to put forth the effort as well as incur the pain of honest feedback in order to develop this type of leadership style. Why? It is probably mostly because of ego. While a lot of managers are willing to put in the effort, very few are willing to receive the negative feedback necessary for them to see themselves as they are and make the necessary changes. This is why there are very few managers who have the leadership skills necessary to effectively turn around a sinking ship.

Peter Tourtellot indicated that he also sees a pattern of management not wanting to deal with tough issues. He said, "This pattern exists because sometimes managers can't stand firing people who have been around them a long time. Sometimes they can't deal with closing certain facilities. This lack of action also occurs because they are sort of married to products, which may have been successful in the past. It is amazing how they can't seem to cut the string."

Most turnaround "experts" are consultants who come in about the time a company files for Chapter 11. At this point, turnaround consultants are managing cash flow and cutting headcount and expenses. I asked Peter Tourtellot why managers wait so long to call in outside help. He said, "I've tried to answer that question and I don't have the answer. I think a lot of it has to do with ego. A lot has to do with them not wanting to admit that they are failing. But mostly, they don't want to admit it to themselves. The trouble is that when we get called many times the patient is in denial. I can't tell you how many times we have said if we were there six months earlier we could have done something."

The goal of an outside consultant at this point is the survival of the business. Survival is about financials. A true fundamental turnaround is about fundamental change. Few consultants are even equipped to deal with fundamental change. That isn't their focus. Their focus is to try to ensure that the company, in some shape or form, will exist in the future.

Sure they make changes to achieve this. Peter Tourtellot indicated that "one of the reasons a turnaround manager is so effective is because he doesn't have any of the emotional attachment baggage."

The changes consultants make are usually "top down"; that is, how do we cut expenses in order to make the cash flow positive? The difference is that these decisions are usually made without the involvement and support of the organization.

Yes, quite often the labor union has to approve the change. The key difference is that the union gets involved in reviewing the proposal and making tough choices. They generally do not get invited to get involved in developing the recommendations as an active partner.

What is the difference? In a word, it is *ownership*! Without ownership, "fixes" are seen as negative cost cutting, which generally has an unfavorable impact upon the workers. By being invited to participate in the solutions, workers and labor unions develop ownership for the proposed changes. Yes, it is *much* more difficult to achieve workable solutions with the involvement of workers and labor unions. Yet without their "buy-in," solutions are generally ineffective.

So many companies looking for solutions are desperate. They are concerned about quick solutions; they think that magic answers will fix their woes overnight. The truth is that there aren't any quick fixes, only effective ones. Effective solutions aren't ones that can be developed and implemented overnight. So, go for the effective solutions, not band-aids.

Now, it is time for the *final solution*, the solution that keeps a business out of trouble from the get-go. It isn't magic, it doesn't cost billions of dollars, and it is effective and available to every company. Is this too good to be true? Is it a mirage?

The truth is that if companies actively practiced the principles, leadership characteristics, practices, and philosophies described in this book, they most likely wouldn't be in need of a turnaround. They would be successful most of the time. The principles mentioned in this book can and should be actively practiced before a turnaround is needed.

The best way to avoid being in a survival situation is to manage and lead your organization every single day in the same manner you should manage and lead your organization in a turnaround situation. Good, effective leadership will generally protect an organization from having to look down the jaws of extinction. While outstanding leadership cannot always overcome all of the potential circumstances that can sink a business, it can overcome most of them.

Don't wait for the wolves to be at your doorstep before you start leading and managing in order to engineer a turnaround. Start now! Don't wait; go out and do it! Leading an organization this way will keep you from having to lead and manage in a crisis. Managing in a crisis is much more difficult, stressful, and energy sapping than leading a successful organization in the same way.

Why then don't more leaders and managers lead and manage this way? It is because they don't know how. CEOs, COOs, and general managers lead and manage in the way that they think will be effective. The truth is there are very few role models out there from which they can learn. This is because very few business leaders have successfully gone through the painful turnaround learning experience. Since most turnarounds are "engineered" by outside consultants, the learning isn't passed on from one management generation to another. As a result, managers tend to manage from their experience and learning. If their experience doesn't include turning a business around, then their management experience will be much different, and their leadership and management style will reflect that fact.

The challenge then is to convince managers that they need to change their skills and styles even though their businesses aren't in trouble. The issue is, **why should they**? The answer is because **waiting until your company is in a terminal condition is often too late.** What is being done isn't working. My favorite definition of insanity is expecting different results by doing the same thing. If we don't change the way we lead and manage, why should we expect a different result?

The choice is ours. So far, the vast majority of the leadership of American companies has chosen to continue to lead and manage in the same traditional ways. Yes, some companies have made terrific progress, but most have not. This isn't about winners and losers. **If America cannot maintain its capability to manufacture our key**

products and supplies, it will have an apocalyptic impact on our economy. This is why we must change and change now.

Finally, if you do have to engineer a turnaround, there is no other feeling like it in the world. Knowing that you have saved an untold number of jobs is, in itself, an awesome feeling. Think about the number of employees who will be comforted by the job security, the regular paychecks, and the knowledge that their future is more secure. Think of the quality of life that you have preserved for your people.

The other indescribable feeling is watching your people grow and develop. You watch them at first fret, sweating and pale with uncertainty. You give them all the encouragement, coaching, and support you can. Seeing them develop into highly effective leaders and mangers, confident of their ability and proud of their accomplishments, produces an indescribable feeling. It is one that makes the sleepless nights, missed meals, dusty workout equipment, and frustrated spouses worth it all.

Chapter Twenty-Six
Workbook

- What are the principal differences between managing by wandering around and getting involved?

_____

_____

_____

_____

_____

- Being a participative manager is critical to turning a business around successfully. How do you know if you are an effective participative manager or not?

_____

_____

_____

_____

_____

- Are you committed to becoming an intensely involved, participative manager? If so, what sacrifices are you willing to make to achieve this goal?

_____

_____

_____

The Ten Turnaround Commandments

1. You cannot cost reduce enough in order to save the business. If that's all you do, you will fail.

2. Don't judge people by what they say or even just by what they do. The best way to assess commitment is to judge them by what they don't do.

3. Commitment is much more powerful than control.

4. Unless you know where you want to take your business, you will never get there.

5. To turn a business around, you must achieve accountability for performance from the very top of the organization all the way down to the very bottom.

6. Not all margin percents are created equal.

7. Just because a business is making a good profit doesn't mean it is well managed or well led.

8. You must personally manage the two top lines, sales and cost of sales, in order to improve your bottom line.

9. Segment your businesses and your costs. If you don't, you will never achieve your maximum potential.

10. Making good quality is a reflection of management's attitude about it.

Appendix
Team-Building Tools

Survival Exercise: Snow Storm

The purpose of the paper "survival" exercise is for participants to learn the value of "group think" and working together in a collaborative manner with an exercise that is very interactive.

The Situation

Your hiking party decided to spend the day hiking in a remote part of the Rocky Mountains. A sudden and ferocious snowstorm caught your party far from your four-wheel drive vehicle. While the trek back to the vehicle was difficult and extremely cold, everyone made it back without any injuries or frostbite.

Your attempt to drive out of the wilderness failed, as a huge rock that was hidden by the drifting snow tore out the transmission. Fixing the four-wheel drive vehicle and making it drivable is impossible. The engine and ignition systems still work. You have about a half a tank of gas, which will run the engine for about five to six hours.

You hear on the radio, which is still working, that the snowstorm is a major one and is not expected to end for at least 24 hours. Immediate clearing, however, is then expected. Temperatures tonight are expected to plummet below zero with winds in excess of 50 miles an hour. The high temperature tomorrow, before the expected clearing, is zero with a continuation of the high 50 mile an hour winds.

While you have a vague idea of where you are, you are unsure of your exact location. Your best guess is that you are about 50 miles from the nearest paved secondary road. Upon checking the one and only cell phone, you discover, to your horror, that it is dead, and you do not have another battery. Your four-wheel drive vehicle has standard equipment with buckets in the front and a continuous back seat. A spare tire is in the storage area. All windows are glass.

A quick check of the storage area finds the following items: two old blankets, some hubcaps, a snow shovel, a sheath knife, a first-aid kit, a shot gun with a box of shells, two boxes of crackers, a map of the area, and a magnetic compass. Everyone is wearing hiking boots and a wool jacket and has sunglasses. Collectively you find $3.50 in change and $100 in bills. In the glove compartment you find various assorted maps.

In taking inventory to access your survival possibilities, your group has compiled a list of 15 items. Your task is to rank them from the most important (1) to the least important (15) in terms of your survival.

You are to assume that:

- All members of your party have agreed to stay together.
- The number of your party is the same as the number of your group.
- The time is 1:00 PM. Your families expect you back by 8:00 PM and have a vague idea of where you are.

Individual Work Sheet

Below are listed the 15 items your group has compiled. Your task is to rank them according to their importance to your survival. Place the number one by the most important, the number two by the next most important, and so on through number fifteen, the least important.

___Two boxes of low sodium crackers

___Blankets

___Cigarette lighter (no one has any matches)

___First-aid kit

___Gasoline

___Hoses

___Hubcaps

___Car mirror

___Knife

___Magnetic compass

___Map of the area

___Shotgun (with shells)

___Snow shovel

___Spare tire

___Sunglasses

Do not allow more than 20 minutes for the individual team members to rank these items. If they get finished earlier, then immediately get started on ranking these items as a group. Do not assign a team leader. Tell them that they have 45 minutes to discuss the ranking and decide as a group.

Once the group rankings are finished, compare the correct answers (see following) to each individual's ranking. Give the correct answer for number one and the explanation. Have each member record the correct ranking next to his or her original ranking for each item. Next, have each member subtract the correct ranking number from his or her original ranking number for each item.

For example, if the correct rank was three and the individual's rank was five, there would be a variance of two (do not use pluses and minuses, just the variance value). Then, have everyone add up the numeric total of the variances (the lower the total, the higher the score).

Have everyone call out their total and list them on a flip chart.

Next, grade the group rankings and total their variances. Unless there is a survival expert in the group, the total of the group variances should be lower than the lowest individual total.

Correct Answers

In this survival situation, there are three life-threatening problems:

- Death from exposure can occur in a few hours.
- Death from dehydration can occur in three days.
- Death from starvation can occur in one to three weeks, depending on physical exertion, exhaustion, etc.

1. **Knife.** The most pressing survival need is to insulate your body against the cold. The primary technique to accomplish this is to create dead air space around your body. The knife can be utilized to cut up the seats and remove the padding for use as insulation inside your clothing.

2. **Two Blankets.** Heat flows from warm to cooler surfaces. Any areas of the body left unprotected allow heat to be conducted away from the body. Two blankets, cut with the knife, can be utilized to form makeshift hats and gloves.

3. **SUV mirror.** While signaling during the snow storm is impossible, a small mirror is the single most effective signaling device. In sunlight, its reflection can reach beyond the horizon.

4. **Cigarette Lighter.** The lighter can be used to start a fire. Besides warmth, fire is the most effective night signal.

5. **Gasoline.** This is the best fuel available for a fire. It can be siphoned with a water hose.

6. **Hoses.** They can be used to siphon gasoline.

7. **Hubcaps.** You cannot eat snow without causing dehydration. To survive for any period of time, you must melt the snow first. The best implement for doing this are the hubcaps bent into the shape of a pot.

8. **Spare Tire.** It can easily be ignited if deflated, and if soaked with gasoline, it will make a good signal, throwing off black clouds of smoke.

9. **Sunglasses.** Once the weather breaks, the reflection of the sun off the surface of the snow can cause snow blindness within one day.

10. **Shotgun.** Other than fire, it is the only other effective night-signaling device. Three shots in rapid succession is the international distress signal.

11. **Crackers.** While death from dehydration would occur long before death from starvation, since you would have plenty of drinking water, eating would ward off physical exhaustion and would produce body heat.

12. **Snow Shovel.** A snow cave is warmer than a car, which conducts heat into the atmosphere. While it isn't recommend that you try to dig out a cave in a snow-storm, it can be used after the storm stops.

13. **First-Aid Kit.** Besides fixing scrapes and bruises, the creams provide useful protection against the sun.

14. **Map of the Area.** This is worthless except as fuel for the fire.

15. **Magnetic Compass.** Potentially the most dangerous item you have because it may encourage someone to actually try and walk out into the storm. It is doubtful anyone could survive the two nights that would be spent trying to get to the road.

Learning

If the total of the group variances is lower than the lowest individual score, it means that synergism gave the group a better chance for survival. This would demonstrate that while group consensus and decision making takes longer and isn't efficient, it is more effective. Management must be focused on effective decision making, thus the value of teams. If a team member's score is lower than the group's score, it would indicate that the team member didn't properly influence the group with his or her knowledge. By avoiding conflict, the group member would have endangered the team by not being assertive.

Group Discussion:

1. Did the team talk strategy (i.e., stay versus trying to walk out) or did they try to rank the items without a strategy? If they didn't develop a strategy, what prevented them from doing so?

2. How did they decide the rankings? Did they vote or reason it out? Which is more effective?

3. Did the group learn that group concensus, while time consuming, is a much more effective way of making critical decisions?

4. How will your team go about making decisions?